About the Author

Robin Sampson

Robin Sampson is a home schooling mother of eleven, grandmother of twelve, and author of several acclaimed books including *What Your Child Needs to Know When*, *A Family Guide to the Biblical Holidays*, and *The Heart of Wisdom Teaching Approach*.

Robin has been writing and speaking, covering a broad spectrum of home school topics, from education philosophies to Biblical studies for over fifteen years. Robin has authored articles for magazines such as *Homeschool Today*, *Teaching Home*, *Home School Digest*, *The Old Schoolhouse*, and *Restore Magazine*.

Robin actively lives her subject as she continues to home-educate her youngest children. Several of Robin's children are grown, married, and homeschooling their own children. Robin's husband, Ronnie, is a deputy director for Homeland Security in Washington, D.C. They reside in northern Virginia.

WISDOM
An Internet-Linked Unit Study

By Robin Sampson

Heart of Wisdom Publishing
http://HeartofWisdom.com

Disclaimer

Heart of Wisdom is nondenominational, functioning entirely apart from any denominational agenda. The main objective of our unit studies focuses on students and parents learning God's Word and establishing a relationship with Him.

Many biblical scholars with varying doctrinal opinions and positions are considered by the author to be qualified to contribute to particular areas of research. This book contains research and/or recommended resources by men and women of various denominations—Messianics, fundamentalists, Jews, etc.—in cases where the author believes that they are biblically correct in their area of expertise and in their investigation and presentation of the truth. This does not mean that the author or publisher are in complete doctrinal agreement with all authors of contributed scholarly text or recommended resources.

Wisdom: An Internet-Linked Unit Study
ISBN: 0-9701816-6-3
Copyright May 2004
Reprint July 2004
All rights reserved.

Heart of Wisdom Publishing
146 Chriswood Lane
Stafford, VA. 22556
540-752-2593

Web site: http://HeartofWisdom.com
E-mail: Support@HeartofWisdom.com

Printed in the United States of America

Dedication

To my sweet, loving Grandmother,
Edna Ellis

Thank you for showing me wisdom's path.

What Others are Saying About
the *Wisdom Unit Study*

The *Wisdom Unit Study* exceeded our expectations. Our son is 14. I have already recommended the study to several families. There were several things that we liked about the wisdom study. The study was very well organized, making it extremely "user friendly." In particular I appreciated the way it facilitated personalizing the study. The introduction to each lesson and the variety of possible activities/projects was extremely helpful. Not only did the study help my son with his research and writing skills, I saw spiritual growth and maturity in him as well as in myself.
—Cindy Pearson

Everyone I talk to tells what a bargain Heart of Wisdom studies are. My goodness, in *Wisdom* alone I have downloaded enough web sites to be well worth purchasing a book that costs $40-50...worth its weight in gold.
—Kathy Kin, Family Bookshelf

I was thrilled to find the *Wisdom Unit Study*. It was what we needed to set our priorities straight and get back in balance. Thank you so much for your hard work. We love the links and the writing helps!
—Debbie Thomas

I can't tell you what a blessing the *Wisdom Unit Study* has been to our family. It's just what we needed to get back on track. We had drifted from our original goal to teach our children God's ways. Our focus switched to academics, logic and Latin—of all things! The children really enjoy the lessons and look forward to them. We've all really enjoyed the Bible tidbits you link to on the Internet. I feel like I am now following God's way and the burden has been lifted! It is true, His burden is light. When I stopped pursuing the world and got the right focus, school became much easier. God bless your work.
—Maria

We are currently doing the *Wisdom Unit Study* and I absolutely think it is outstanding. I would highly recommend HOW to anyone who has been intimidated by the preparation involved in doing unit studies. Robin has done a wonderful job in selecting resources...Every family who does the study will flavor it with their own character, so no two families will do it exactly the same---for instance, Robin suggests reading from an alternative resource called *Heart of the King* each day; some families might not order it, but we did and each

day we do ONE verse and it has sparked such intensive conversation between the kids and me that we can spend nearly an hour on that part alone!
Heart of Wisdom is a provision of God to my family. I can't tell you the number of time s I have cried as it has ministered to my heart, how many times I have thanked God for a "curriculum" that integrates what I believe so strongly about education into one package, that it gives me a fleshed-out skeleton to trim or add to as He leads, and still leaves me time to be a mother.

I tried doing unit studies before and while the kids loved them and learned from them, I was worn out by keeping up with planning and trying to locate/substitute books that were no longer in print or carried by the library. The fact that HOW puts God's Word in its proper position of preeminence is the best part. It is natural to it, like breathing and so my kids are being bathed in it constantly. Since God's Word is living and powerful and they are bathing in it, I expect to see some beautiful fruit.
—Liz Fenstemaker

I love the *Wisdom Unit Study*! We have homeschooled for 9 years and this is the best study we have experienced. Robin has developed an excellent Bible-based study and I appreciate her work so much.
— William Canant

We started the *Wisdom Unit Study* about a month ago...my daughters are 15 and 17. Since we started using Heart of Wisdom several years ago, guess who's learned the most? *That would be me!!!* Yes, my girls have learned much, too, but I am mostly convinced that God brought HOW into our lives to teach me, and the Wisdom unit is no exception. It's not that I didn't learn any of what's in there before, but it is so well-organized and in-depth that I am re-learning and being added to with its content. Plus, it is so timely with all the major (and minor) decisions in our lives this year. I am working ahead in the unit on my own and so appreciating its input in my life. It is an amazing unit study and I am so thankful for its part in "our" curriculum.
—Heart of Wisdom Customer

Using HOW has been a life-changing experience for our entire family. We spend more time together in God's Word and are growing in our understanding together! Learning Israel's history has been a tremendous benefit to understanding all of history, past, present, and future. Also, learning about our Hebrew roots has brought new

Wisdom unit and are gleaning so much already. I know that God orchestrated HOW becoming part of our homeschooling.—anonymous

We have loved it so far, though we are moving slowly through the material for greater retention of the truths. We have only been using the materials for one month. I believe HOW is an answer to prayer and it has been a great blessing to my family. We are using *Creation* and *Wisdom Unit Studies* currently. We are only a few lessons into it and already my 14 year-old is planning to put a Creation Science Club together in order to encourage/teach others the truth of a literal, six-day Creation and its foundational importance.

The units are teaching ME so much. The *Wisdom Unit Study* has been very convicting and has led to many precious and invaluable discussions with my children. —anonymous

I so appreciate the ease of use and the fact that HOW can be used in the way God leads a particular family using it. Because of this ability to flex to the family and be individualized, HOW keeps learning engaging and interesting rather than dry. Thank you Robin for all of the hard work you've put into HOW!—anonymous

I must say I'm thankful for this unit study, I realize that I am lacking wisdom and that the path I am on is definitely not going to lead me to it! So if I'm not on the correct path, how can I lead my children down the correct path? The answer is simple...I can't. I must first change the direction of my path and, like little ducklings follow their mama, my children will follow me...This unit study is worth its weight in gold; not only will your children benefit from it, your whole family will benefit from it.—Merrilee Defoe, *Eclectic Homeschool*

My parents bought the *Wisdom Unit Study* for me (I'm 16!) and in the nearly three lessons that I've done already, I am absolutely blown away!! Wisdom just has so much to it—and the extra books recommended are pretty heavy stuff too! But seriously, I doubt that there would be another unit of this depth and intensity as this one. Wisdom is just the best, and I've learned heaps!! Thank you so much for putting this out!— Iona

This unit study looks awesome. .. I have gone through much of the material and can highly recommend its use in the homeschool as well as for youth groups in a congregational setting or family devotional type learning setting. I really was bowled over when I saw the material I received for the money I paid. This was a real bargain in value learned versus value spent. —Debra Lynn

My husband and I were highly satisfied and impressed with the *Wisdom Unit Study*. This is the first HOW unit study that we have used so far, and we are just finishing it now. We thought it was quite comprehensive, without being "bogged down" or over-done. We were especially impressed with the wealth of suggested resources, and, of course, the Internet Resources —WOW! Thank you, thank you, thank you for doing such a thorough job! It really communicated to me, who has been a homeschooling mom/teacher/disciple for 9 years that you seem to truly care about this, rather than just putting something together to sell.—Janis Leal

The *Wisdom Unit Study* is wonderful. I am getting through it slowly but I have enjoyed it so far. My children are 13, 9, 6, and 2 but I am using the study right now for myself. It has really made me think. I have loved the reading so far. I have read through and thought about things that I have just skimmed over in the past. I think this is a great study not just for children but for the adults. I have learned so much for myself. I also plan on doing the other studies as well. — Karen M. in Florida

The *Wisdom Unit Study* exceeded my expectations. It is a great development of a worldview. The material is well presented and flexible...I am education co-ordinator for Spirit of Truth and we have made this unit a key unit in our core curriculum. The curriculum is excellent in its development of a Christian worldview.—Iain Belot

The *Wisdom Unit Study* blessed our socks off! We decided as a homeschool family that this was the first unit study we would start with. Since that time, the Lord has used the wisdom that He has given us through His Word, to minister to young adults. Since our move to Plano, we are part of a church where we are the only homeschoolers...We went through the *Wisdom Unit Study* with our children ages 7, 10, 15, and 16. The younger children listened, helped read aloud, answered some questions, and had their input as the Lord led. It is great to see that you have put a package together for the study...The internet sources are incredible.—Leo and Eileen Karlin

I did the *Wisdom* study along with *Adam to Abraham* and *Creation* this year. I am homeschooling three of my boys ages 9, 15, & 17... my 9 year old also enjoyed quietly listening to our conversations while we did this study. For those parents who use this, I would just recommend a private prayer time alone before teaching each lesson, because the material covered and the lessons learned are the most important for a parent to discuss with a child, especially older children who will soon be making their own decisions. I have to echo those that say this study is an answer to prayer... Be warned, once you start, you won't want to stop to study anything else! —Janine

Add your comments at **http://Homeschool-Books.com**

Recommended in: ◆ several lessons in this unit; ● several HOW unit studies ◐ Key Resource for this unit.

Wisdom
An Internet-Linked Unit Study

Table of Contents

Key to Symbols 8

Interacting with the Internet 9

Scheduling and Teacher Helps 12

The Four Step Lessons 13

Unit Overview

Wisdom Overview 16

Wisdom Objectives 18

Wisdom Vocabulary 19

Wisdom Resources 20

Lessons

Choosing the Wise Path 26

Worldly Wisdom 33

Benefits of Wisdom 39

Acquiring Wisdom 43

Studying God's Word Wisely 47

Obeying God's Word 61

Praying for Wisdom 70

Managing Conflict Wisely 75

Seeking Wise Counsel 80

Dealing with Temptation Wisely 86

Wise Relationships 92

Wise Goal-Setting 99

Wisdom Literature 105

Wisdom of Solomon 111

The Ultimate Wise Relationship 115

Works Cited 122

Key to Symbols

Resource Symbols

 Book or magazine

 Key resource

 Internet site

 Resource recommended in several Heart of Wisdom unit studies

 Audio resource

 Resource recommended in several units planned for the same year

 Resource suitable for all ages (read-aloud)

 Resource recommended in several lessons in a unit

 Video or television program

Activity Symbols

 Writing assignment

 Add to Time Line Book, make a chart, or make a graphic organizer

 Vocabulary or make a list

 Expand research

 Copy passages; outline; fill in a worksheet

 Think and discuss

 Listen

 Write a letter

 Map work

 Prepare a meal or recipe

 Create artwork

 Experiment

 Contrast and compare

Interacting with the Internet

The Internet is an open door to an enormous, exciting library. The wealth of information on the Internet can be overwhelming because a search for a single topic can lead to thousands of links; but Heart of Wisdom units guide you to the best and most appropriate Web sites to enhance each lesson. You can go quickly to the links from **http://Homeschool-Books.com.**

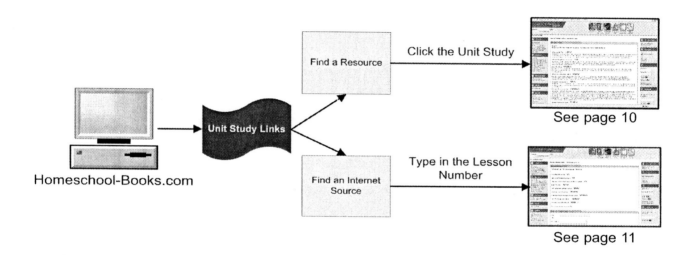

To access the links, you need

- A PC with Windows 95 or higher, or a Macintosh PowerPC/Power Mac with Mac OS 8 or higher;
- A browser such as Internet Explorer (IE) or Netscape (we recommend IE);
- A connection to the Internet by either modem or cable;
- An account with an Internet Service Provider (such as AOL or MSN);
- For some content, you may need a "plug-in" programs such as RealPlayer, QuickTime, or Shockwave, which allow you to play audio or video files. There is usually a button that enables you to download any necessary plug-in(s) at no charge.

Recommended in: ◆ several lessons in this unit; ♥ several HOW unit studies ☀— Key Resource for this unit.

Resources Listed by Thematic Unit Study

When unit studies first became popular in the homeschool market, resource suggestions were a big problem. Many times the resources were hard to find or out of print. Our Internet links solve this irritating problem. Go to http://Homeschool-Books.com and click on FIND A RESOURCE. Simply click on the link to go to the online vendor carrying the product. Alternative books are listed for any books that go out of print. The resources on our site are listed alphabetically and marked by grade level K-3 4-8 9-12.

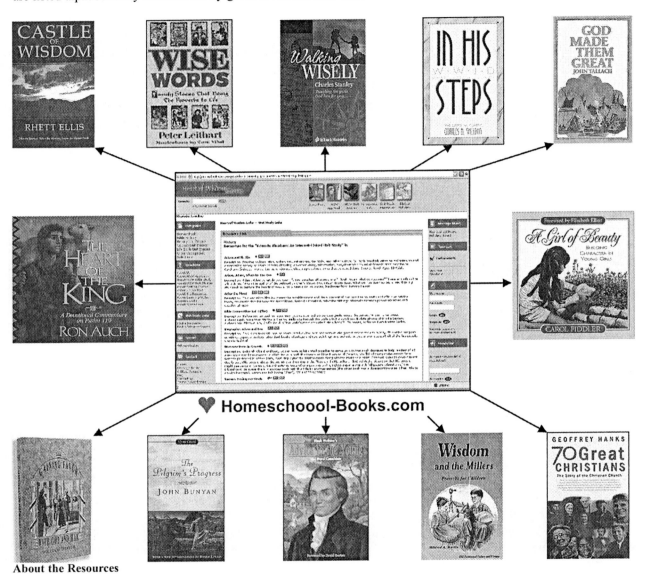

♥ Homeschoool-Books.com

About the Resources

The suggested resources are completely optional. This unit study includes so many links to information on the Internet you can use this unit without referring to any additional resources. However, students need to read (and feel and smell) real books! We have included several resources that are popular with homeschoolers so you can utilize what you have on hand. You are going to make two investments in your homeschool: time and money. Investing in good resources will save time. Utilizing the library and inter-library loan will save money. Each family will need to consider the resources they need based on their homeschool budget, time available, the number of children that will be using this program, and their personal interests.

Internet Links Listed by Lesson

Links are available to maps, articles, Bible studies, video clips, photos, audio files, worksheets, instructions, interactive lessons, etc., which are appropriate sites for any given lesson. To access the proper links, go to http://Homeschool-Books.com and click on FIND AN INTERNET SOURCE. Type in the Lesson Code (example: H10102) to view the links. Sites are marked by appropriate age level K-3 4-8 9-12.

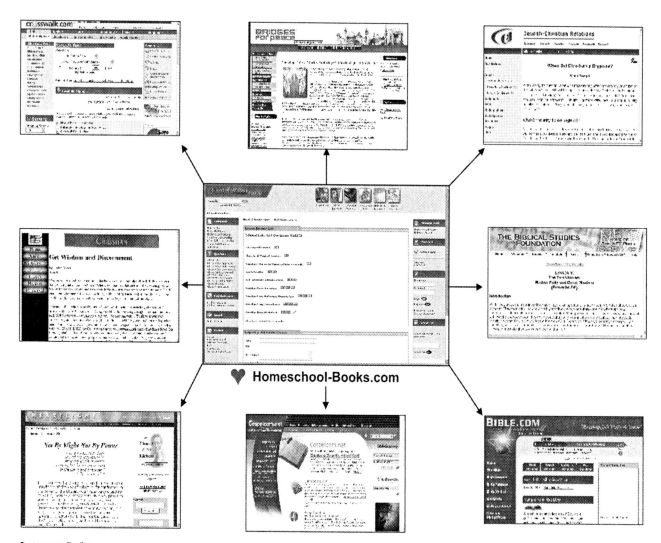

♥ Homeschool-Books.com

Internet Safety
The computer can be a wonderful tool, but also a great temptation. We suggest that you view all sites with your children or, at a minimum, have your computer in an easily seen area in your home (never in a child's room or turned away from parental eyes). Typing in long URLs can mistakenly lead to undesirable sites. We recommend that you use **http://Homeschool-Books.com.** to go directly to the applicable sites and avoid typing in URLs.

Site Availability
URLs for Internet sites change, and sometimes sites go offline completely. HOW links are continually updated with new links, new resources, and alternatives to dead links. Occasionally, you may get a message that a site is down. This usually means that the server is busy and you can try again later.

Recommended in: ◆ several lessons in this unit; ♥ several HOW unit studies ☞ Key Resource for this unit.

Scheduling and Teacher Helps

Pray for guidance as you plan your schedule. Only God knows the needs of your individual child. The time you spend on each lesson will depend on the level of your student(s), your resources, and the activities you choose.There are sixteen lessons in this book; you can complete one lesson a day for a three week study or expand the lessons over several weeks or months. Remember your main goal is in Matthew 6:33, *"Seek ye first the kingdom of God, and His righteousness, and all these things shall be added unto you."* There are four steps in each lesson, and you should touch on each step in each lesson. The average time for each step is:

- **Step 1:** Five to ten minutes to discuss the lesson.
- **Step 2:** Thirty minutes to an hour to research and read sections in the resources (several hours for high school students, or longer if the student is extremely interested in the subject).
- **Step 3:** Thirty minutes to two hours to complete each assignment or project.
- **Step 4:** Up to an hour to correct and share work (or ten to twenty minutes if only sharing).

Important: Do not skim or skip Step 1. *Spend time discussing the questions with your child.* This step baits the hook in order to catch the fish. It activates prior knowledge, creates interest, generates focus, and whets appetites. It is an essential anticipatory set with direct relevance to the instructional objectives that secures the attention and interest of the learner. This step engages the student by relating the material to his or her own life and experiences. Traditional schools dive right into a subject (Step 2). Studies show that 70% of children do not do well beginning with Step 2. Step 1 establishes continuity with previous lessons, finds out what a child already knows about the topic, transmits learning expectations, and makes the new material relevant.

One of the best ways for a student to understand a topic is to write or talk about it. Using these processes, students will comprehend the material, restructure the new information, and then share their new understanding. Writing and narrating assignments are both about learning and creating new ideas. In each lesson during Steps 3 and 4, younger students should be able to tell you in a few sentences (narration) what the lesson was about. You can write down the narration to include in the students' portfolio. Older students should either copy passages, or complete writing assignments. During these assignments, students learn how to assess information and determine its appropriateness, how to evaluate and compare, analyze and discern, add their own feelings, organize information, and communicate conclusions. Students develop excellence in achievement by producing the required quality assignments; they develop diligence by continually practicing clarity, accuracy, relevance, prioritizing, consistency, depth and breadth through writing activities. They retain the material longer and practice writing mechanics at the same time.

Essential Teacher Helps

For more details about the Heart of Wisdom Teaching Approach, instructions for creating various notebooks, guidelines for correcting written work and worksheets, go to our Internet site at http://Heartofwisdom.com/Helps.htm or see our book *The Heart of Wisdom Teaching Approach*, soon to be available from http://Homeschool-Books.com.

- ❤ Bible First Philosophy
- ❤ Delight-Directed Studies
- ❤ Charlotte Mason Methods
- ❤ Learning Styles and Four Step Lessons
- ❤ Writing to Learn
- ❤ Correcting Written Work
- ❤ Multi-Level Teaching
- ❤ Creating a Portfolio
- ❤ Creating a Time Line Book
- ❤ Creating a Vocabulary Notebook
- ❤ Creating a Spelling Notebook
- ❤ Graphic Organizers
- ❤ Worksheets

The Four Step Lessons

Each lesson in this book contains four basic steps. These four steps are a cycle of instruction based on the four learning styles identified in *The 4Mat System* developed by Dr. Bernice McCarthy. Each of the four steps teaches to one of these four learning styles. This cycle of learning is based on the fact that different individuals perceive and process experiences in different, preferred ways; these preferences comprise our unique learning styles. Studies show that this four-step method motivates students to comprehend the material better and retain the information longer.[1] Students become comfortable with their own best ways of learning, and grow through experience with alternative modes. The chart below gives an overview of the four learning styles.

Type 1	Type 2	Type 3	Type 4
A Type One learner is one who perceives concretely and processes by thinking through an idea. Type Ones are "people" people. They learn by listening and sharing ideas and by personalizing information. They need to be personally involved and seek commitment. They tackle problems by reflecting alone and then brainstorming with others. They demonstrate concern for people. They excel in viewing concrete situations from many perspectives and model themselves on those they respect.	A Type Two learner is one who perceives abstractly and processes actively working with an idea. Schools are made for these types of learners. They are eager learners who think through ideas. They are thorough and industrious, and excel in traditional learning environments. They are excellent at discerning details and at sequential thinking. They tackle problems rationally and logically. They are less interested in people than concepts.	A Type Three learner is one who perceives abstractly and processes by thinking through an idea. Ninety-five percent of the engineers tested are Type 3. They excel at down-to-earth problem solving. They are common-sense people. They have a limited tolerance for fuzzy ideas. They experiment and tinker with things. They tackle problems by acting (often without consulting others). They need to explore, manipulate, and experience things to understand how things work.	A Type Four learner is one who perceives concretely and processes actively working with an idea. These types of learners seek to influence others. They learn by trial and error. They are self-discovery learners. They thrive on challenge. They adapt to change and relish it. They tend to take risks and are at ease with people. They perceive things with emotions and process by doing. They need to be able to use what they have learned.

Studies show that seventy percent of children do *not* learn well the way the schools teach—lecture/textbook/test—most students need more. Traditional schools use mainly linguistic and logical teaching methods relying on classroom and book-based teaching, repetition, and exams for reinforcement and review. Those who do well under these circumstances are labeled "bright" or "gifted." Those who learn differently can easily be labeled "learning disabled" or "dumb." By recognizing and understanding your child's learning styles, you can use techniques better suited to them improving speed and quality of their learning.

The most important thing to realize about learning styles is that one style is not better than another. We all have different intellectual strengths. No one fits into a box; we are all unique individuals created by God. Each of us is a combination of the four types, more or less, in one or two categories. The Bible teaches that we are all different parts of the body of Christ and that one part is no better than another part (1 Corinthians 12:12-25).

1. For more on this subject see: *Learning Styles: Reaching Everyone God Gave You to Teach* by Marlene D. LeFever, *4Mat System: Teaching to Learning Styles With Right-Left Mode Techniques* by Bernice McCarthy, *4Mat in Action* by Susan Morris and Bernice McCarthy; *About Learning* by Bernice McCarthy and Carol Keene (Illustrator) and HeartofWisdom.com/LS.htm.

Recommended in: ◆ several lessons in this unit; ◑ several HOW unit studies ◑— Key Resource for this unit.

The Four Step model consists of four instructional goals:

1. Motivating students
2. Teaching ideas and facts
3. Experimenting with Concepts & Skills
4. Integrating new learning into real life.

It addresses four styles of learners:

1. Those who learn by listening and sharing ideas
2. Those who learn by conceptualizing — integrating their observations into what is known,
3. Those who learn by experimenting—testing theories in practice
4. Those who learn by creating—acting and then testing their new experience

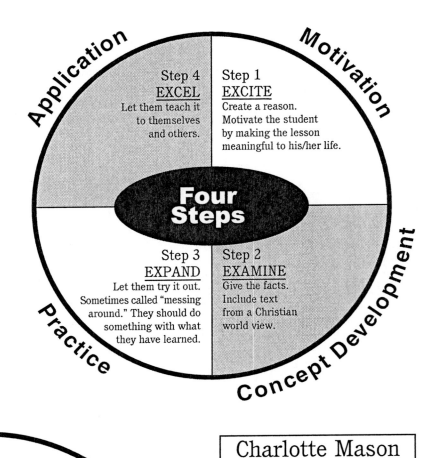

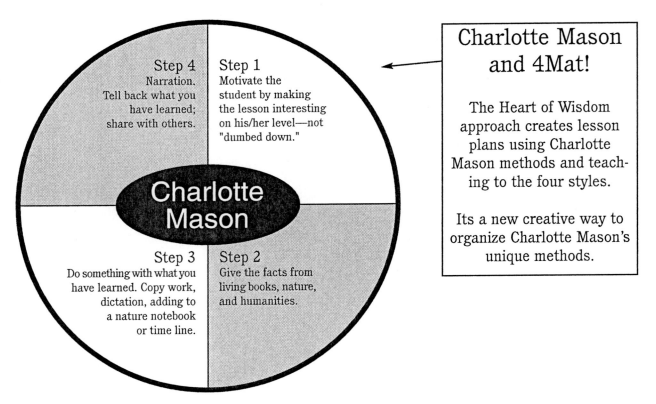

Charlotte Mason and 4Mat!

The Heart of Wisdom approach creates lesson plans using Charlotte Mason methods and teaching to the four styles.

Its a new creative way to organize Charlotte Mason's unique methods.

Education in Bible Times

Step 4
Israel was to instruct all nations in divine holiness and redemption as Yahweh's instrument of light to the nations.

Step 1
Motivation—Israel's mandate was to diligently teach their children to love God, and to know and obey his statutes and ordinances (Deut 6:1-9).

Step 3
Oral and written recitation. Repetition in observation, experiential learning (doing), listening, reciting, and imitating.

Step 2
The aim of education was ethical and religious, centering on the Torah and recognizing and remembering events of divine providence in history.

Modern-day science may have come up with the 4 Step System, but is it really a new way to teach or have we had this pattern all along?

The 4 step lessons are designed so that all learning styles are addressed, in order that more than one type of student may be permitted to both "shine" and "stretch." Each lesson contains "something for everybody," so each student not only finds the mode of greatest comfort for him/her, but is challenged to adapt to other, less comfortable but equally valuable modes.

How Jesus Taught

Step 4
He asked them to go and tell others. "Go ye therefore, and teach all nations..."

Step 1
He took the people where they were and made the lesson meaningful to their lives in some way. He spoke to shepherds about sheep, farmers about planting, fishermen about fish, etc.

Step 3
He asked them to do something with what they learned—to actively respond—doing and practice are vitally connected with knowing.

Step 2
He brought in the facts—Scripture, "It is written,..."

Recommended in: ◆ several lessons in this unit; ● several HOW unit studies ●— Key Resource for this unit.

Wisdom Overview

"Wisdom" to most people means academic ability, but the Bible views man as a unified whole, never separating academic learning from spiritual wisdom.

A Parable

Once upon a time there was a village far away in a remote location, which had experienced a hard year of severe weather. A group of missionaries worried that the villagers' crude huts would not be able to withstand the strong weather any longer. The missionaries wanted to help by taking supplies to the village, but there were no accessible roads for a car trip and there was no landing field for a plane.

The missionaries decided to have a small plane air-drop supplies over the area until they could get there themselves. They sent food and tools (shovels, saws, hammers, screws, screwdrivers, etc.). The missionaries hoped that the villagers would use the tools to build new homes sturdy enough to resist the rough weather.

It took several months to repair the necessary roads to get to the village. Once the missionaries arrived, they noticed that the villagers had rebuilt the same crude handmade huts. They were surprised to see tools tied on the tops of stakes about eight feet tall in front of each new hut. The tools were badly rusted and had never been used. Instead of working with the tools to build new homes, the villagers worshiped them. The tools became a status symbol. The villager with the most tools hung over his hut was viewed with awe and admiration.

In this parable the tools represent education. Academic subjects studied in school and colleges are tools meant to help a person in life. A Christian should use the tools to better himself to become the person God wants him to become—a wise person. When one has an unbalanced view of education, the tools are viewed as the end result instead of an apparatus to reach the goal. A diploma on a wall or the ability to spout facts is not wisdom. The ability to speak several languages or read philosophical literature is not wisdom.

In this book, you will learn that true wisdom is understanding and knowing God. The moment we understand and know God, we begin to see His holiness. We see His purposes, His love for man; we know who God is, so there's never any hesitation to obey Him. Scripture often uses the words *knowledge*, *understanding*, and *wisdom* interchangeably, but occasionally they are spoken of as though they are separate and distinct. Thus, it may be useful to attempt to define the differences in their meanings: *Knowledge* is recognition of the facts, *understanding* is the ability to lift the meaning from the facts, and *wisdom* is knowing what to do next.

Those with knowledge are able to collect, remember, and access information. They "know" the Scriptures. God's Word is literally "in them." They are scholars. However, it is possible to have knowledge and lack understanding and wisdom; that is, you may have the facts but have no clue as to their meaning or what to do with them.

Those with understanding are able to extract the meaning from information. They "see through" the facts to the dynamics of what, how, and why that is being conveyed in the information. They are teachers. Understanding is a lens that brings the facts into crisp focus. Understanding produces rules of thumb, or principles.

Those with wisdom know which principle to apply, and when. Understanding without wisdom can appear contradictory. For example, "He who hesitates is lost" is as valid a principle as "Haste makes waste." We see the truth in both, but we wonder which we should apply in our current situation. Those with wisdom know what to do next. They know which way to go. They do the right thing. In contrast, there are many who have great knowledge and understanding, but consistently do the wrong thing. Wisdom, in this sense, is the goal, and knowledge and understanding only have eternal value as they result in wisdom or help us to do right.

The cover of this book depicts two paths. In life's journey we have the choice to take either the wise or the unwise path. The results of walking wisely are joy, peace, contentment, confidence, and being in the presence of God. The results of walking unwisely are conflict, discouragement, disappointment, disillusionment, and discontentment. Jesus taught that there are two paths:

> *Enter by the narrow gate; for wide is the gate and broad is the way that leads to destruction, and there are many who go in by it. Because narrow is the gate and difficult is the way which leads to life, and there are few who find it.* (Matt. 7:13–14)

God has called us to walk wisely. Situations arise in daily life for which the Bible does not supply a specific checklist of answers. In these situations we need to ask, "What is the wise thing for me to do?" Paul commanded the believers in Ephesus to live wisely.

> *See then that ye walk circumspectly, not as fools, but as wise, Redeeming the time, because the days are evil. Wherefore be ye not unwise, but understanding what the will of the Lord is.* (Eph. 5:15–17)

We are to think things through, to look at things from every angle. Believers are to show concern in decision making, finances, relationships, business transactions, family issues; indeed, in everything. What is wise for one may not be wise for all. God guides the believer in the way of wisdom. To refuse to live wisely is to ignore His leading. According to Proverbs, the wise man has length of days, long life, peace, and prosperity. God desires that we walk wisely so we can become the persons He created us to be and accomplish the work He has called us to do.

Teaching Mutli-Ages?

This book was written for grades 7-12 but we included resources for younger children to benefit families with several ages. If you are using this book with younger children, the lessons will require reading aloud and simplified explanations for the younger grades.

Recommended in: ♦ several lessons in this unit; ♥ several HOW unit studies ☛ Key Resource for this unit.

Wisdom Objectives

Upon completion of this unit, your student should:

- Understand the true meaning of wisdom

- Understand how to obtain wisdom

- Understand the difference between worldly wisdom and God's wisdom

- Comprehend basic Bible study techniques

- Study the lives of wise people in the Bible

- Apply Scripture personally

- Discover the characteristics of a wise person

- Acquire principles for making wise choices

- Comprehend the effects of excluding God from education

- Understand the pitfalls of money and how to make wise financial choices

- Perceive the purpose of the Law

- Understand the significance of our Hebraic roots

- Grasp that obedience is a key to walking wisely

- See an example of godly training

- Understand the differences between wisdom, knowledge, and understanding

- Find out about the lives of contemporary men and women of wisdom

- Learn about Solomon and his wisdom

- Understand the importance of studying God's Word in order to be wise

- Learn about ancient Israel and its relevance to today

- Understand reasons and principles for setting goals

- Study portions of the Book of Proverbs

- Understand the foolishness of sinful anger and how to avoid it

Wisdom Vocabulary

See Vocabulary Instructions on our web site.

access	dependable	judge	resolve
accountable	determine	judgment	responsible
acrostic	distinguish	judicious	restraint
affect	endurance	knowledge	rhetoric
alertness	erudition	logic	scrutinize
allegory	establish	metaphor	self-control
allusion	estimate	motif	self-discipline
ambition	evade	myth	sensible
analysis	evaluate	narrator	serenity
appraise	exegesis	objective	shrewd
ascertain	explanation	occurrence	similarity
assume	facts	parallel	simile
astute	fear of the Lord	parallelism	simple
attentiveness	fortitude	patience	sophistication
awareness	futurist	penalty	study
block logic	genre	perception	suppose
canon	goal	perceptive	survey
clever	hedge	personification	synonym
cliché	hermeneutics	poetry	target
common sense	idiotic	ponder	thoughtless
comprehension	imagery	presume	tolerance
conclude	imprudent	prevaricate	Torah
conscientious	inclusion	prophet	understanding
consequences	indecisive	prose	vacillate
consider	infer	proverbs	verify
contemplate	influence	prudent	waver
context	information	pseudepigrapha	will power
culture	insightful	purpose	wisdom
cunning	intellect	reason	wisdom literature
decide	intelligent	renaissance	wise
deduce	investigate	research	worldly wisdom
deliberate	irrational	resemblance	

Recommended in: ♦ several lessons in this unit; ♣ several HOW unit studies ☜ Key Resource for this unit.

Wisdom Resources

This study was designed for grades 7–12; *however*, we want encourage families with children of all ages to study this topic so we included resources for grades K-12. The resources listed here are entirely optional and provided merely for your convenience. Any of these resources will help you or your children grow in wisdom. A very important part of teaching your student to love to learn is making available interesting resources. It is also enormously valuable for your student to acquire essential study skills such as pulling together information from several different resources (particularly when researching Bible topics).

Resources with a ☞ are the most pertinent resources for this unit study. Resources with a ◆ would be useful in several lessons in this unit study. Resources with a ♥ are suggested in several Heart of Wisdom Unit Studies. Approximate grade levels are indicated with the following symbols: K-3 4-8 9-12 . Resources are listed alphabetically.

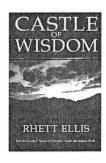

Castle of Wisdom by Rhett Ellis 9-12
This is a very interesting little book that reads like a fairy tale and is very difficult to put down. I began reading the book aloud to our children and quickly found that it contained some things that I was not ready to discuss with my younger children (ages 7 and 9). I did complete the read with my teenager, however, and it made an impact. The book is about Elias, a curious young man, who sets out to find the "Castle of Wisdom," a mysterious old ruin where he believes he will learn The Master Truth: The meaning of life, the secret of existence, the reason for it all. Along the course of his eighteen-year journey, he experiences everything from romance, joy, and wealth, to misery, pain, and poverty. Because he is dealing with life, he encounters many seedy subjects, including some sexual situations and homosexuality (my reason for not recommending it for all ages). The story is a parable about seeking God's Word. It's full of symbols and occasionally poetic. I strongly recommend it for older students. Paperback - 142 pages (December 1999). Sparkling Bay Books; ISBN: 0967063108.

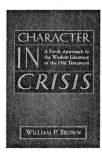

Character in Crisis: A Fresh Approach to the Wisdom Literature of the Old Testament by William P. Brown 9-12
This study demonstrates that the aim of the Bible's wisdom literature is the formation of the moral character of both individuals and the believing community. Brown traces the theme of moral identity and conduct throughout the Old Testament. Paperback - 179 pages (February 1996). Wm. B. Eerdmans Publishing Co.; ISBN: 080284135X. Reading level: high school.

Gaining Favor With God and Man by William Thayer 4-8 9-12
An 1893 classic, this essential addition to your household library of forgotten, valuable Christian heritage classics will enrich your family legacy as you glean from these ageless republished accounts of men and women who were representative of purity in biblical standards, Christian character, and noble achievements. Thayer asks how honored Americans reached greatness. He

answers his own question by saying, "Each possessed character, a noble purpose, ability to do, courage to dare, industry, perseverance, and patience, or waiting for results." Includes character-building subjects such as: Courage, Decision, Idleness, Modesty, Honesty, Keeping Promises, Keeping a Diary, Perils of Success, The Bible in Business, and over 100 additional short subjects. The book is currently in its 7th republished edition. People have written Heart of Wisdom to say that this book has been a tremendous tool for family devotions. Numerous classic lithographs; good read-aloud. Hardcover - 446 pages (January 1989). Republished by Mantle Ministries; ISBN: 1889128384. Reading level: junior high through adult. Best for family reading aloud.

A Girl of Beauty by Carol Fiddler **4-8**
Foreword by Elisabeth Elliot. Author and mother Carol Fiddler urges parents to accept their God-given authority and the high privilege they have to turn undesirable situations around by correcting their daughters' behavior and requiring accountability for the truth. Written especially for preteens, A Girl of Beauty addresses issues such as truthfulness, sincerity, service, respect and contentment. Each chapter includes questions to guide girls in applying the truths taught and provides Scriptures to read for further study and guidance. The foundational truths presented in this book will serve as a starting point of discussion, application and further training specific to your daughter's circumstances and idiosyncrasies. Chapters: Character Building, Truthfulness, The Key to Success, Sunshine-Makers, Sincerity, Careful Words, Keeping Confidences, Ideals, Ambition, A Sense of Purpose, Service, Personal Presentation, Courtesy and Respect, Loyalty, Competition, Disappointments, Meditation, Contentment, and Besetting Faults. Written for girls 8 to 12. Back to the Bible; (August 2000) ISBN: 0847414280

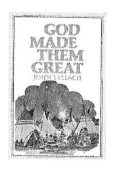

God Made Them Great by John Tallach **4-8** **9-12**
Who is the greatest in the kingdom of heaven? The Lord Jesus set a child in front of his disciples to answer this question. John Tallach sets the simple, child-like faith of five Christians before us in order to show us true greatness in God's kingdom. In vivid style he describes their varying backgrounds, their conversion experiences, and the resulting faith and zeal seen in their self-giving service to others. Excellent biographies, recommended especially for ages nine to sixteen, but suitable for readers and listeners of all ages. Paperback, 135 pages (June 1982). Banner of Truth; ISBN: 0851511902.

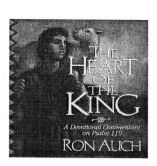

The Heart of the King by Ron Auch **4-8** **9-12**
A devotional commentary on Psalm 119, this is an excellent book to use through the course of your wisdom study. Read aloud one devotion per day as you begin your day in prayer. As you study the life of David you will quickly find that it is outlined with a deep love and affection for God. David also had a strong prayer life. He meditated on God's love and did not hesitate to seek the Lord's wisdom. Hardcover - 192 pages (March 1995). New Leaf Press (Master Books); ISBN: 0892212780.

Recommended in: ◆ several lessons in this unit; ● several HOW unit studies ◉— Key Resource for this unit.

In His Steps by Charles M. Sheldon `4-8` `9-12`
A ragged man tells a Midwestern church congregation, "It seems to me there's an awful lot of trouble in the world that somehow wouldn't exist if all the people who sing such songs went and lived them out." The man later passes away. The minister and congregation are shocked and ashamed and proceed to pledge to live their everyday lives asking themselves, "What would Jesus do?" Asking, "What would Jesus do?" is the same as asking, "Is this a wise decision?" This is the book that started the WWJD movement. This is a superb book to read aloud and discuss with your children. Paperback - 256 pages (December 1993). Barbour & Co; ISBN: 1557483469.

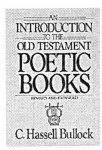

Introduction to the Old Testament Poetic Books by C. Hassell Bullock `9-12`
The five books known as the "poetic books"—Job, Psalms, Proverbs, Ecclesiastes, and the Song of Solomon—are unique in that they focus on man's reflections on God and God's response, rather than on God's search for man. They are also referred to as wisdom literature, particularly the books of Proverbs and Ecclesiastes. Dr. Bullock writes, "The individual and personal nature of the books that we undertake to study is evidence of the attention given in the Old Testament to the importance of the individual to God." Dr. Bullock offers an in-depth study of each of these five books, including: hermeneutic considerations, literary structure, authorship and provenance, purpose and meaning, doctrine and theology, canonical considerations, and poetic structure. Hardcover (August 1988). Moody Press; ISBN: 0802441416. Reading level: high school or adult.

Noah Webster's Advice to the Young by Noah Webster `4-8` `9-12`
This book contains two historical reprints which founder Noah Webster wrote to "enlighten the minds of youth in religious and moral principles and restrain some of the common vices of our country." Promoting honesty, generosity, gratitude, and more, these works are invaluable today for all ages. (Foreword by David Barton.) Paperback - 53 pages (August 11, 1996). Wallbuilder Press; ISBN: 092527934X.

Our Father Abraham: Jewish Roots of the Christian Faith by Marvin R. Wilson ♥ `9-12`
The chapter "The Contour of Hebrew Thought" is a superb explanation of a Biblical view of wisdom.. Although the roots of Christianity run deep into Hebrew soil, many Christians are regrettably uninformed about the rich Hebrew heritage of the church. This volume delineates the link between Judaism and Christianity, between Old and New Testaments, and calls Christians to examine their Hebrew roots. Upon completion of this book you will: understand the importance of reading and interpreting Scripture from the context in which it was written; see the sixty-six books of the Bible telling the same story, not thirty-nine books (Old Testament) telling one story, and twenty-seven books (New Testament) telling another; have a general understanding of the 1st Century believers and how Christianity became separate from Judaism. Paperback - 374 pages (April 1989). W. B. Eerdman's Pub. Co.; ISBN: 0802804233. Readings from this book are recommended in several Heart of Wisdom studies.

Pilgrim's Progress by John Bunyan 9-12
Join Christian and his companions on their journey to the Celestial City, as they pass through many experiences common to us all, in Bunyan's timeless allegory of the Christian's walk with God. Mass Market Paperback - 299 pages (April 2, 2002). Signet Classic; ISBN: 0451528336.

Proverbial Wisdom and Common Sense by Derek Leman 9-12
A Messianic Jewish approach to today's issues from the Proverbs. This virtual encyclopedia of practical advice from Scripture tackles vital issues, such as family relationships, sexual morality, finances, reputation and gossip, laziness and diligence -- and more! It portrays wisdom as uncommon because it often the opposite of our natural inclinations. Wisdom says the way up is down (that is, through humility), the way to rule is to serve (just as Jesus came to be a servant to all), the way to live is to die (that is, dying to selfishness, pride, greed, lust, etc.) Our natural desires attract us to pleasures of sex, food, wine, and easy living, but wisdom says otherwise! Proverbs 21:17, *He who loves pleasure will become poor; whoever loves wine and oil will never be rich.* This book contains: a compilation of sayings on love, money, laziness, dieting, anger, etc; insights from rabbinic and Messianic Jewish sources; a ten minute a day devotional plan for grasping the book and its wisdom; practical applications for each day's topic; New Testament references to Proverbs' principles. Paperback 248 pages. ISBN: 1880226782.

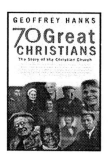

70 Great Christians: Changing the World by Geoffrey Hanks 4-8 9-12
From the first century to the present, Christians have been changing the world! In this fascinating account of the lives of seventy Christians, you'll discover how belief in Jesus inspired ordinary people to accomplish extraordinary things. From Paul to Martin Luther, Elizabeth Fry to Corrie ten Boom, you'll be moved by their courage and strengthened in your own spiritual journey. Includes plenty of pictures, maps, and charts. Paperback - 342 pages (1993). Published by Christian Focus; ISBN: 1871676800. Reading level: high school or read-aloud.

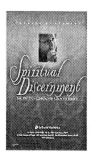

Success God's Way by Dr. Charles Stanley 9-12
A study book. Do you know what it takes to be successful? Does it require money? or fame? or is there another way? God's definition of success has nothing to do with fame or fortune—real success revolves around a relationship with Jesus Christ. In this life-changing book, Dr. Stanley reveals the true meaning of success and the scriptural principles required to achieve it. Take steps today toward becoming the person that God wants you to be. Hardcover - 256 pages (February 2000). Thomas Nelson; ISBN: 0840791429.

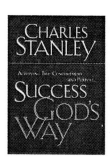

Walking Wisely Study Kit by Dr. Charles Stanley 9-12
What does it mean to be wise? The world says that wisdom comes with age and experience. But the Bible says that wisdom begins with the reverence of the Lord. Do you live wisely? How can you tell? In this study kit, Dr. Stanley shares the meaning of wisdom, how to acquire it, how it will bless you, and how you can walk wisely. The *Walking Wisely Study Kit* includes four hours of teaching on two video cassettes, plus a sixty-four-page workbook packaged in a keepsake binder. Available from In Touch Ministries: http://Intouch.org or (800) 789-1473.

Recommended in: ◆ several lessons in this unit; ✿ several HOW unit studies ☛ Key Resource for this unit.

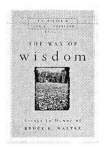

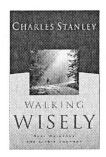

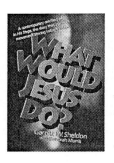

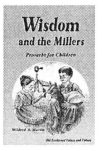

The Way of Wisdom by J. I. Packer, Sven Soderlund 9-12
This book was written in tribute to Dr. Bruce Waltke for his seventieth birthday. It is an insightful collection of writings exploring the wisdom perspective of the Bible by nineteen of his colleagues. Wisdom has defined Dr. Waltke, both as one of his personal qualities and as the core of his many years of biblical study, invoking the highest efforts of his formidable intellect and etching itself indelibly on his character. This book displays a level of scholarship and insight in keeping with Dr. Waltke's high academic standards, and a breadth of outlook reflective of his own broad grasp of God's Word and its application to all of life. Highly recommended. Hardcover - 272 pages (2000). Zondervan Publishing House; ISBN: 0310227283. Reading level: high school or college.

Walking Wisely: Real Guidance For Life's Journey by Dr Charles Stanley
⊶◆ 4-8 9-12
In Scripture, wisdom is portrayed as a most important treasure, something to be sought after with consistent discipline. We, as Christians, tend to think of wisdom as something to be attained—an ideal to which we aspire. Dr. Charles Stanley contends that genuine wisdom is evidenced in how we live. The truly wise person is one whose values, perspectives, career goals, and daily decisions are all shaped by the wisdom found in Christ. Choosing to live according to biblical precepts is a lifestyle foreign to the worldly patterns among which we live. Inevitably, there will be clashes between the wisdom of God and that of the world. Dr. Stanley teaches how to apply God's wisdom as we handle finances, relate to others, care for our physical health, and carry out day-to-day duties. This significant volume presents a way of living that embodies wisdom from above. **Note: The order of the lessons in this unit study follows the order of the chapters in this book.** Hardcover - 256 pages (February 5, 2002). Thomas Nelson (Publisher); ISBN: 0785272984.

What Would Jesus Do? by Garrett Ward Sheldon, Deborah Morris 9-12
A contemporary retelling of *In His Steps*, the story that started a movement among today's youth. Paperback - 192 pages (1998). Broadman & Holman Publishers; ISBN: 080540189X.

What Would Jesus Do? by Helen Haidle K-3   4-8
This book presents a variety of situations and discusses how Jesus would behave in each of them, covering such qualities as sharing, living in peace with others, and being truthful. Includes 140 full-color illustrations, plus discussion questions in the back of the book from each of the eighteen chapters. Hardcover - 256 pages (March 1997). Zondervan Publishing House; ISBN: 1576730530. Reading level: ages 4–8. Interest level: all ages.

Wisdom and the Millers by Mildred A. Martin K-3
My children loved these stories! Wisdom and the Millers make Proverbs come alive for children! Here is a character building collection of lively, inspirational stories. Each chapter explains and illustrates a passage from the book of Proverbs, along with a story based on true life experiences. Follow the four "Miller" children as they learn great truths of life and wisdom; sometimes through their parents' stories, and sometimes the hard way! Will a father's prayer keep his family safe from the burglar? Why did Timmy get a bloody nose at the family reunion? And

what is the sad story behind their mother's wooden stool? Read about these, twenty-two other exciting stories. Paperback, 159 pages. A.B. Publishing. ISBN 0962764353.

Wisdom Hunter by Randall Arthur **9-12**
This is an *inspired* novel about the hypocrisy of Christian legalism and a man's search for the only surviving member of his family. This page turner is based on author Randall Arthur's own difficult experiences. The story's hero, Pastor Jason Faircloth, embarks on a journey that lasts eighteen years and takes him through four countries during his quest to find the granddaughter who is being hidden from him. In a process that mirrors our own spiritual journey, he discovers a rich relationship with God and the peace that finally comes with true faith. Paperback - 323 pages (November 1999). Multnomah Publishers Inc.; ISBN: 1576732304. Warning: adult content.

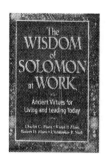

The Wisdom of Solomon at Work: Ancient Virtues for Living and Leading Today by Charles C. Manz, Karen P. Manz, Robert D. Marx, Christopher P. Neck **9-12**
This is actually a book for adults in the workplace; it is included for parents using this study or teens in the workplace. This collection of personal stories illustrates how people today are reconciling spiritual values with modern life, providing a fresh perspective on an age-old debate. It shows how the lessons found in the Old Testament have value in modern daily life, and illuminates the virtues of humanity in each story. Hardcover - 175 pages (2001). Berrett-Koehler; ISBN: 157675085X.

Wise Guys: A Guide to Building Godly Character in Boys by Dan and Carol Fiddler **K-3** **4-8**
True "wise guys" know that wisdom is a gift from God. This book will guide young men in recognizing the difference between the world's wisdom and godly wisdom and urge them to commit to honor God and live for Him above all else. Each of the 16 topics will help boys plug into Scripture in a way that will shape their character, while familiarizing them with key stories in the Bible. 121 pages, Back to the Bible Publishing (2001),ISBN: 0847454061.

Wise Words by Peter Leithart, Toni Wall (Illustrator) **K-3** **4-8**
Noticing the thematic parallels between many biblical stories and fairy tales and unable to find good, biblical bedtime stories for his children, Peter Leithart began writing his own. The result of that endeavor is this finely illustrated collection of eighteen of his best stories. Peter writes, "My intention in *Wise Words* was to write stories that would appeal to children as stories; that would challenge parents who read to their children; that would illustrate biblical Proverbs; and that would borrow imagery, plots, characters, settings, and themes from the Bible." Achieving that, these tales will deepen every family's appreciation for the Book of Proverbs. Written in the tradition of Grimms' Fairy Tales, it is a fascinating storybook that will bring both pleasure and illumination to parents and children. Paperback - 169 pages (January 1997). Holly Hall Pub.; ISBN: 1880692236.

Recommended in: ◆ several lessons in this unit; ● several HOW unit studies ●— Key Resource for this unit.

Choosing the Wise Path LS10101

Step 1: Excite

The Bible uses a literary device called personification to refer to wisdom. *Personification* means "giving human qualities to items that are not human." For example, Wisdom is portrayed as a respectable, proper, and dignified lady. Her ways are open and honest. Lady Wisdom calls to the simple, the foolish, and those most in need of her. Mistress Folly, on the other hand, is personified as an obviously wayward woman. Her ways are secretive and deceptive. This contrast shows us that the search for wisdom and meaning in life can attract us to the wrong path.

You have been invited to a banquet! Lady Wisdom has dispatched her maidens to relay her invitation. She has taken great care to prepare her spacious house ("seven pillars"). She prepares the banquet table and menu with wine and meat.

> *Wisdom hath builded her house,*
> *she hath hewn out her seven pillars:*
> *She hath killed her beasts [butchered her meat];*
> *she hath mingled her wine;*
> *She hath also furnished her table.*
> *She hath sent forth her maidens;*
> *She crieth upon the highest places of the city,*
> *Whoso is simple, let him turn in hither:*
> *as for him that wanteth understanding, she saith to him,*
> *Come, eat of my bread, and drink of the wine which I have mingled.*
> *Forsake the foolish, and live; and go in the way of understanding.*
> (Prov. 9:1–6)

You have received a second invitation, this one from Mistress Folly. Mistress Folly is not the same type of hostess as Lady Wisdom. You won't receive a hand-delivered invitation by a messenger. Mistress Folly sits in her doorway and calls to whoever is within ear shot. Mistress Folly offers stolen water and food in secret.

> *For she sitteth at the door of her house,*
> *on a seat in the high places of the city,*
> *To call passengers who go right on their ways:*
> *Whoso is simple, let him turn in hither:*
> *and as for him that wanteth understanding, she saith to him,*
> *Stolen waters are sweet, and bread eaten in secret is pleasant.*
> *But he knoweth not that the dead are there;*
> *and that her guests are in the depths of hell.*
> (Prov. 9:14–18)

Which invitation will you choose? Have you ever accepted an invitation and and later regretted it?

Think about and discuss an instance in which you made a really good choice even though it was contrary to the peer pressure around you. What helped you to stand up for truth? How difficult was it? What does it mean to "walk in wisdom"? What is this wisdom? What is its aim and origin?

Step 2: Examine

The only way to walk wisely is to seek the Lord. Christians are to "walk in wisdom" as we live out our lives: *See then that ye walk circumspectly, not as fools, but as wise, Redeeming the time, because the days are evil. Wherefore be ye not unwise, but understanding what the will of the Lord is* (Eph. 5:15–17).

Wisdom is the ability to make informed decisions and select the best course of action. Everyone makes poor choices now and then. Sometimes, we give in to the pressures of popular opinion and make decisions we later regret. Describe a situation in which you made a poor choice. What factors led you to make your decision? How do you plan to avoid repeating your mistake in the future?

The Book of Proverbs is one of the books known as "wisdom literature." The words *path* and *way* are found nearly 100 times in the Book of Proverbs. Wisdom is a path to walk. The path of wisdom leads to life, but the way of folly leads to death. How do we find this path? Proverbs chapters 2–4 illuminates the path to wisdom.

> **Proverbs 2** explains how wisdom protects our paths. It includes instruction on how to attain wisdom and how God protects us.
>
> **Proverbs 3** explains how wisdom directs our paths. These verses follow an alternating pattern of commands and rewards, focusing on four commands:
> 1. To trust in God and not lean on our own understanding
> 2. To fear God and not be wise in our own eyes
> 3. To honor God and not fail to give to Him
> 4. To appreciate God and not misunderstand the value of His discipline
>
> **Proverbs 4** explains how wisdom perfects our paths. It explains how wisdom gives life, protection, and honor.

George Barna, an American pollster specializing in observing and recording religious trends, says that modern Christianity is "a mile wide and an inch deep." Mile-wide Christianity is not the path to God's Kingdom. According to Jesus, it is the highway to destruction. Jesus' Sermon on the Mount concludes with a powerful illustration of the narrow way:

> *Enter ye in at the strait gate: for wide is the gate, and broad is the way, that leadeth to destruction, and many there be which go in thereat: Because **strait is the gate, and narrow is the way, which leadeth unto life**, and few there be that find it* (Matt. 7:13–14).

J. E. Smith explains in *The Wisdom Literature and Psalms* that the first twenty-seven verses of Proverbs chapter 14 are designed to help one find the path of wisdom and stay on it. These verses stress the truth that people who pursue wisdom find joy, and those who do not experience sadness:

Recommended in: ◆ several lessons in this unit; ● several HOW unit studies. ●━ Key Resource for this unit.

Heart of Wisdom Publishing   WISDOM   27

1. Focus on the family (14:1). *The wise ones of women* [each] *builds her house.* The term *builds* is used figuratively for building up the prosperity of the family. On the other hand, *folly* [in a woman] *with her own hands tears it down.* The reference is to any activity, however good in itself, which diverts a woman from her number one priority, the family. This verse underscores the tremendous influence of a woman in the home.

2. Fear of Yahweh (14:2). *He who walks in his uprightness fears Yahweh.* Reverence for God motivates and characterizes the righteous lifestyle. One's holy manner of life is evidence that he has been influenced by religious motives. On the other hand, *he whose ways are perverse, despises him.* Perverse ways are sinful ways. All sin is offensive to God (cf. Gen. 39:9). Those who neither fear nor love the Lord make no effort to exercise self-control. Wickedness is proof that one has lost all reverence for God and concern about pleasing him.

3. Wise speech (14:3). *In the mouth of a fool is a branch* [producing] *pride.* Growing conceit, accompanied by insolence toward others, tends to get a person into trouble. On the other hand, *the lips of wise men preserve them.* Such do not abuse speech to insult and injure others. Their words tend to conciliate others, and promote peace and good will. They speak with courtesy and caution and thus avoid potential harm.

4. Hard work (14:4). *In the absence of oxen, the crib is clean.* The owner is thus spared the labor of providing food for the animals or cleaning the area where the animals are normally kept. On the other hand, *great harvests come from the strength of an ox.* This animal was used for plowing and threshing the grain. Without the ox there is nothing to put in the granary. Therefore, the advantages of keeping an ox far outweigh the disadvantages. An investment of time and effort is essential to an abundant harvest.

5. Honest testimony (14:5). *A faithful witness will not deceive.* He cannot be induced to swerve from the truth by threat or bribe. On the other hand, *a false witness breathes forth lies,* i.e., lies pour out of his mouth like breath from the nostrils (cf. 6:19).

6. Search for wisdom (14:6-7). *Should a mocker seek wisdom, then it is not*, i.e., it does not exist for him. Such a one cannot find wisdom because he lacks the essential prerequisite, viz., the fear of the Lord (Ps. 111:10). True wisdom is not to be attained by those who are too conceited to receive instruction, who presume to depend upon their own judgment, and who weigh everything by their own standard. But why would a mocker seek wisdom at all? Perhaps for ulterior motives. He surmises that wisdom would enhance his prestige and position. He does not love wisdom for its own sake, hence he never receives it. On the other hand, **knowledge is easy to the person of discernment.** Spiritual knowledge comes easily to one who realizes that the fear of God is a necessary precondition, and who earnestly seeks it from the hand of the Lord (14:6).

Choosing the right path is not always the easiest choice. But when we choose to do things God's way, we will always be blessed as a result. And we should remember that making wrong choices will always bring a consequence that we may not want in our lives.

Suggested Resources

Below are more resources on choosing wisdom's path.

Walking Wisely ☞ ◆
Introduction and Chapter 1, "The Challenge of God's Word: Walk in Wisdom" (1–12).
You will be advised to read other chapters with upcoming lessons in this book.

Additional Reading

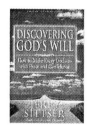

Discovering God's Will: How to Make Every Decision with Peace and Confidence
by Jerry Sittser
We've all heard that God has a plan for our lives, but what does that mean in practical terms—when we're faced with important life decisions, like who to marry, what job to take, where to send our children to school, or what church to join? Sometimes God's perfect will seems difficult to find, confusing to follow, and easy to miss. Discussing these and other questions, Jerry Sittser offers a biblically based approach that readers will find truly liberating. No matter what decisions you've already made, he points out that it is still possible to live out God's perfect will for your life—even if you think you've married the wrong person, chosen the wrong career, or landed yourself in some kind of serious trouble. Includes study questions designed for individual and group use that will be helpful to anyone faced with decisions large and small. Paperback - 256 pages (2002). Zondervan Corp; ISBN: 0310246008. Reading level: high school or adult.

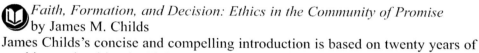

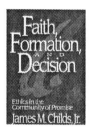

Faith, Formation, and Decision: Ethics in the Community of Promise
by James M. Childs
James Childs's concise and compelling introduction is based on twenty years of teaching and writing in Christian ethics. Illuminating his case with examples from business, medicine, and public policy dilemmas, Childs constructs an original and comprehensive proposal for Christian ethics—dialogical ethics—one that resonates well with contemporary concern for character and virtue, but is also animated and informed by Christian faith. Paperback - 166 pages (June 1992). Fortress Press; ISBN: 0800625005. Reading level: high school or adult.

Seven Steps to a Quality Decision by Buddy Harrison
Has God ever given you a dream that has caused you to be so excited that you were not able to sleep at night? Then, as time passed without the dream becoming a reality, you may have lost your enthusiasm in pursuing that dream. Perhaps you even question whether it was from God in the first place. Many times our dreams do not become reality because of the decisions we make in our lives. In this book, Buddy Harrison outlines God's pattern for making quality decisions. Whether your decisions are "spiritual" or "natural," these steps will help you achieve the desires, goals, and dreams that God has given you. Paperback - 80 pages (2000). Harrison House; ISBN: 0892747366. Reading level: high school or adult.

Recommended in: ◆ several lessons in this unit; ♥ several HOW unit studies. ☞ Key Resource for this unit.

Video

Making a Decision Last Forever

Making a commitment to Jesus Christ . . . it's the most important decision you'll ever make. Your eternal destiny is at stake. For many people, this decision fades into a less-than-life-changing commitment. They become as the prophet Hosea said *"those who perish for a lack of knowledge."* (Hos. 4:6). *Making a Decision Last Forever* examines the foundational truths upon which a lasting decision is based. These are hard-hitting but humorous lessons that can be studied and practically applied to the viewer's life. Whether you're a new Christian, interested in becoming one, or renewing your commitment and faith in Christ, this series will inspire you to a life of victory. Order from American Portrait Films at (800) 736-4567, or http://www.amport.com

Internet Sources

The Narrow Way
A pastor's sermon outline on the narrow way.
http://www.abundantbiblestudies.com/Documents/Bible_Studies/Narrow_way.htm
http://www.corrytonchurch.com/outlines/04252001PM.htm

The Narrow Way Bible Study
This study covers "the strait gate and the narrow way."
http://www.abundantbiblestudies.com/Documents/Bible_Studies/Narrow_way.htm

What Is Wisdom and Why Follow Its Path?
A Bible study from TwoPaths.com.
http://www.twopaths.com/introduc.htm

Step 3: Expand

Choose and complete one or more of the following activities:

Activity 1: Research
Read Proverbs chapters 2, 3, and 4. Here you will see the ways to wisdom's path. Mark the eight responsibilities listed below in your Bible or copy the references into a notebook.

1. Receive (accept) God's Word.
2. Hide God's Word in our minds and hearts.
3. Incline the ear.
4. Apply the heart.
5. Cry after knowledge.
6. Lift up the voice for understanding.
7. Seek for wisdom.
8. Search after wisdom.

Activity 2: Write Summaries
Read Proverbs chapter 2. Write a summary for each of the three different walks described in this chapter: 1) walking with God (vv. 1–9); 2) walking with the wicked (vv. 10–19); and 3) walking with the righteous (vv. 20–22). Refer to "Writing Summaries" in *Writers INC*.

Activity 3: Write an Essay
Name five characteristics of evil and five characteristics of good. Write a two-page essay on what makes a person a good person. Give examples from the Bible. Refer to "Structure of the Traditional Essay" and "Sample of a Traditional Essay" in *Writers INC* or *How to Write an Essay* at http://HeartofWisdom.com/Writing.htm

Activity 4: Make a Chart
Remembering that there is always a consequence to bad choices, copy the following list in your Portfolio. Next to each entry in the list, write down as many possible negative consequences as you can think of. When you have finished, review the list with all the consequences added. Are there any of these choices that are worth the possible results? Discuss.

Stealing	Gossip
Fighting	Cheating
Lying	Drinking
Experimenting with Drugs	Premarital Sex
Homosexuality	

Activity 5: Make a Chart
Read Numbers 11:1–12:15. When Israel left Sinai, three incidents occurred which were truly "examples" for Israel (1 Cor. 10:11). Israel was about to make a vitally important decision—one that would affect the future significantly. God dealt severely with the people at fault in these three incidents. Each was a lesson in responsibility. Each involved unwise decisions and a rejection of God, and each was the occasion of immediate judgment. Make a chart with a summary paragraph for each of the three unwise decisions and the results.

Activity 6: Write a Summary
Read the Book of Esther in the Bible. Write and present a summary of the decision she had to make. Include things such as how she came to her decision, the advice she received, what possible consequences there could have been, and the final outcome of her decision. Keep in mind that Esther was not a middle-aged adult. She was a young girl by our standards of today. As young people, God has equipped us to make right choices for his kingdom.

Activity 7: Contrast and Compare
Read Proverbs 9:1–6. Fill out a Contrast-and-Compare Worksheet about Lady Wisdom and Mistress Folly. Use adjectives to describe the character of each woman. Describe the results of attending or rejecting each banquet. http://HeartofWisdom.com/Worksheets.htm

Recommended in: ◆ several lessons in this unit; ● several HOW unit studies. ●— Key Resource for this unit.

Heart of Wisdom Publishing WISDOM 31

Step 4: Excel

The Bible says that fear of the Lord is the beginning and indeed the essence of wisdom (Job 28:28; Ps. 111:10; Prov. 1:7, 9:10). Most people go through life as if it were a river; they are carried along by the current and pushed from one place to another, going to wherever the river empties. What direction do you choose? Do you make wise decisions or do you allow life to drag you along with its dangerous current, pulling you away from God? Have you made Jesus Christ Lord of your life?

Prayer and Bible study are the first steps to walking wisely. Write a prayer, asking God to help you walk wisely. Seek His face for wisdom. Be like Solomon and ask for wisdom as part of your life experience. Pray that God will help you develop the ability to make righteous decisions. Share your prayer with your parents.

We cannot do right without thinking right—and we cannot think right without learning God's Word. You have to know God's Word to make wise decisions. Plan on spending time on Bible study daily. Ask God to open His Word to you and to make it real in your life. Then walk by the light which that Word sheds on your path.

Correct all written work to demonstrate correct punctuation and spelling, and effective use of grammar. Add corrected written work or any illustrations to your Portfolio. Add new words you learned in this lesson to your Vocabulary Notebook.

Worldly Wisdom LS10102

Step 1: Excite

Education is a course of action that develops one for life. Education influences every area of human experience. The way we see our world, the values we hold as important, the skills we feel are necessary, our opinions of the past, present, and future—all are clearly affected by our education and our educational views. In the last lesson you learned that there are two ways to walk in this world: wisely and unwisely. In our world, however there are different views of wisdom.

Secular Americans usually think of wisdom from a Greek view. The ancient Greeks pursued wisdom in the light of human reason and logic without God. But God's people, the ancient Hebrews, pursued wisdom in the light of divine revelation.

Spend some time now discussing these questions: How do you think one receives wisdom? Is wisdom the same as education? Would a college degree make someone wise? How do worldly wisdom and godly wisdom differ? Is it possible to operate in worldly wisdom without operating in the wisdom of God? Discuss the traits of a wise man.

Step 2: Examine

Paul, in his first letter to the Corinthians, asked:

> *Where is the wise? where is the scribe? where is the disputer of this world? hath not God made foolish the wisdom of this world? For after that in the wisdom of God the world by wisdom knew not God, it pleased God by the foolishness of preaching to save them that believe.* (1 Cor. 1:20–21)

The first search for wisdom in the Bible resulted in sin:

> *Now the serpent was more subtle than any beast of the field which the LORD God had made. And he said unto the woman, Yea, hath God said, Ye shall not eat of every tree of the garden? And the woman said unto the serpent, We may eat of the fruit of the trees of the garden: But of the fruit of the tree which is in the midst of the garden, God hath said, Ye shall not eat of it, neither shall ye touch it, lest ye die. And the serpent said unto the woman, Ye shall not surely die: For God doth know that in the day ye eat thereof, then your eyes shall be opened, and ye shall be as gods, knowing good and evil.*
>
> *And when the woman saw that the tree was good for food, and that it was pleasant to the eyes, and a tree to be desired to make one wise, she took of the fruit thereof, and did eat, and gave also unto her husband with her; and he did eat.* (Gen. 3:1–6)

Satan promised Eve, "Your eyes shall be opened"—that she would have much more of the power and pleasure of contemplation and a larger compass in her intellectual views, and see further into things. He spoke as if she was short-sighted in comparison to what she could be. Partaking of the tree of the knowledge of good and evil did not bring godly wisdom. It brought guilt, fear, and separation from God.

Recommended in: ◆ several lessons in this unit; ◕ several HOW unit studies. ◕━ Key Resource for this unit.

Eve was attracted to the fruit's alluring promise of wisdom. She had to decide whether to believe God or the serpent. Adam chose to believe the woman rather than the loving Creator who had given him the freedom to choose to obey (1 Tim. 2:14). Adam's and Eve's sins are only examples of sin; all of us sin (Rom. 3:23). We have the same decision to make. We are offered the choice between the wisdom of the world and the wisdom of God.

Doesn't the Bible say that knowledge will "pass away"(1 Cor. 13:8)? Isn't it "incomplete"? Doesn't it "puff up"(1 Cor. 8:1)? And then there's the sin involved with the "tree of knowledge" (Gen 2:9). But we are also told to "look for," "ask for," "seek" it, and "walk in" knowledge. How long will knowledge be useful? Brainstorm and discuss: Is there a kind of knowledge that is to be avoided? Is there a type of knowledge that is to be sought after?

> "Wisdom" is the biblical term for this *on-earth-as-it-is-in-heaven* everyday living. Wisdom is the art of living skillfully in whatever actual conditions we find ourselves. It has virtually nothing to do with information as such, with knowledge as such. A college degree is no certification of wisdom—nor is it primarily concerned with keeping us out of moral mud puddles, although it does have a profound moral effect upon us. (Peterson, E. H. 1995)

Worldly wisdom is limited. It is characterized by turmoil, disorder, and selfishness. Brainstorm and discuss some examples of worldly wisdom. The Bible tells us that it's not what you know, but whom you know. In 1 Corinthians chapters 1–4, *wisdom* (Greek, *sophia*) is the viewpoint from which a person deals with the issues of life. Humans are "foolish" when they fail to realize that their ideas must line up with God's divine Word. Only when a person abandons what seems to be wise by the world's standards and accepts God's viewpoint as revealed in Scripture can he or she be truly wise.

Almost anyone can gain the necessary scholastic achievement to become a doctor or a businessman, etc. But is it truly achievement if they become a crooked doctor or businessman? What good is it to know five foreign languages if one does not have tongue control? What good is it to read Greek literature if one does not know the Proverbs of Solomon? What good is it to be proficient in accounting if one cheats on income taxes? What good is it to know the meaning of every word on the SAT vocabulary list if one does not know how to give a kind word?

Education is important. But our main goals should be higher than facts and worldly knowledge. As explained here in a quote from *Gaining Favor with God and Man* by William Thayer:

> Self-control is an everyday necessity. We need it 'every hour,' as we sing of the Savior Himself. The young of both sexes, now qualifying themselves in the schoolroom for the higher and more responsible duties of life, need its constant ministrations. They will not need arithmetic or algebra at all times and in all places, but they will need this cardinal virtue. It may be well for them to learn the names of all the bones of the human body, but it will be of vastly greater service for them to have their powers under complete control. They will need the latter morning, noon, and night, from this time until the close of life, while the former will be of use only at certain times and in certain places.

Thus saith the LORD, Let not the wise man glory in his wisdom, neither let the mighty man glory in his might, let not the rich man glory in his riches: But let him that glorieth glory in this, that he understandeth and knoweth me, that I am the LORD which exercise loving kindness, judgment, and righteousness, in the earth: for in these things I delight, saith the LORD. (Jeremiah 9:23–24)

In the pursuit of knowledge, many people often leave out wisdom. In our achievement-oriented society, significance or importance is equated with intellectualism. Even Christians tend to evaluate worth on the basis of achievement scores instead of who we are in Christ.

Paul dealt strongly with the Corinthians' worldly wisdom. See 1 Cor. 1:17–25; 2:6–16. He affirmed that Christ is the true **wisdom of God** (1 Cor. 1:24).

Knowledge changes with the times and seasons. Wisdom does not. For example, our knowledge of computers today will be old news in ten, twenty, or thirty years. It will be considered ancient history in fifty years. Why? Because technology will increase and get better, and our current systems will be outdated. Our knowledge in these areas will change. But godly wisdom will always remain. It was wise in the day of Jesus' earthly ministry to obey your parents. It still is today. It was wise in His day to seek God's kingdom first, and it still. Godly wisdom in one's life will create a value system that encourages godliness, self-control, kindness, and so on. In short, it will produce character in your life. Knowledge can never do that.

In short, true education should not only teach skills and tasks that make students more knowledgeable. It should instill values and wisdom that will create a lifetime of wise decisions and choices. Your life is a series of choices. There are good choices and bad ones. Wisdom will lead you to good choices. Deuteronomy 30:19 says this: *I call heaven and earth as witnesses today against you, that I have set before you life and death, blessing and cursing; therefore choose life, that both you and your descendants may live...*Godly wisdom helps us to choose life every time.

Read Ephesians 1:17, 1 John 5:20, and John 17:3. Those who are deliberately ignorant and actively avoid truth are the simple. Read the following verses: Ephesians 5:17; James 1:5; Proverbs 1:28–33; 8:11; 9:6; 19:8; 13:20; 23:23; and 24:5–6.

1 Corinthians 3:18–20 sums up worldly wisdom for us. It says:

> *Let no one deceive himself. If anyone among you seems to be wise in this age, let him become a fool that he may become wise. For the wisdom of this world is foolishness with God. For it is written, "He catches the wise in their own craftiness", and again, "The Lord knows the thoughts of the wise, that they are futile."*

Suggested Resources

Below are more resources on the differences between worldly wisdom and godly wisdom.

Our Father Abraham ♥
Chapter 14, "A Life of Learning: The Heart of the Jewish Heritage" (278–315).

Recommended in: ♦ several lessons in this unit; ♥ several HOW unit studies. ☞ Key Resource for this unit.

📖 *Walking Wisely* ⚬━ ◆
Chapter 2, "Earthly Wisdom versus Godly Wisdom" (13–36). You will be advised to read other chapters with upcoming lessons in this book.

Additional Reading

📖 *Assumptions That Affect Our Lives* by Christian Overman
The visible actions of people are first shaped by invisible thoughts, deep in the unseen world of the human mind and heart. What factors influence those invisible ideas? For people who live in the Western world, the answers can be found by examining the two major roots of Western thought—the ancient Greeks and the ancient Hebrews. *Assumptions That Affect Our Lives* takes the reader back to the roots of the modern conflict between Christianity and secular humanism through a comparison of ancient Greek and Hebrew culture. What the reader will discover is that the current tension between evangelical Christians and the non-biblical ideas with which they are surrounded is an age-old conflict. By viewing the current situation in the context of the ancient Greeks and Hebrews, contemporary Christians can be better equipped to deal with the challenges of living in a predominately Greek-based culture today.
Paperback - 273 pages (1996). Micah 6:8 Publishing; ISBN: 1883035503.

Internet Sources

ⓘ The Two Ways (Proverbs 1:7-33)
Article from the Biblical Studies Foundation.
http://www.bible.org/docs/ot/books/pro/deffin/prov-03.htm

ⓘ The Two Women: Madam Folly and Dame Wisdom (Proverbs 7-9)
Article from the Biblical Studies Foundation.
http://www.bible.org/docs/ot/books/pro/deffin/prov-04.htm

ⓘ The House That Wisdom Built
Sermon from www.livingbiblestudies.org
http://www.livingbiblestudies.org/study/JT49/017.html

Step 3: Expand

Choose and complete one or more of the following activities:

🗂 Activity 1: Do Research
Find worldly wisdom at work today. Using newspapers, magazines, and other news and entertainment sources, find ten examples of worldly wisdom. Make a display of the clippings and stories you have located by using a poster or project board. Summarize each of the ten entries and explain why they are good examples of worldly wisdom.

Activity 2: Write a Paper
Write and present a one-page paper on worldly wisdom. Use both biblical examples and resource materials.

Activity 3: Write a Summary
Read 1 Corinthians 1:20–23, James 3:13–18, and Colossians 2:8, and write a summary of these verses. Refer to "Summary Writing" in *Writers INC* or see "How to Write a Summary" at http://HeartofWisdom.com/Writing.htm

Activity 4: Watch the News
With your parents, watch the news each night for a week. Write down any examples of worldly wisdom that are covered in the evening news. How do you think the exercise of godly wisdom would have changed the outcome of the news story? Discuss these events with your parents.

Activity 5: Write a Paper
Do research and write a paper titled "Why the Hebrews Were Poor Philosophers." Refer to *Assumptions That Affect Our Lives* by Christian Overman (pages 143–149).

Activity 6: Write a Paper
The single most important educational gain in America in the last fifteen or twenty years has been the fact that thirty to forty million Americans have learned how to use a personal computer. Brainstorm and make a list of the pros and cons of the computer. Also brainstorm and make a list of the pros and cons of television. Write a two-page paper about the change television has made in the daily lifestyles of Americans. Contrast and compare the changes television has made with the changes the personal computer has made.

Activity 7: Write a Story
Write a fictional story of what education will be like in the year 2020, assuming that the state continues to deny God's existence. If possible, include factual charts showing the decline of the SAT from 1960 until today. Then add fictional data to your story. Refer to "Guidelines for Shaping a Subject" in *Writers INC* (minimum 500 words).

Activity 8: Write a Plan
Become the Secretary of Education for a day. Draw up a very detailed plan of how you would bring public education back into line with strong biblical lessons, morality, and so on taught in the classroom. If the educational system changed today, allowing godly wisdom to be included in classroom instruction, what would you change first? What kinds of units and lessons would you include daily, monthly, yearly? Include these kinds of changes in the plan you draw up. Be sure to include changes for grades K through 12.

Step 4: Excel

Do a Bible study to see if you can find at least one example of worldly wisdom in the Bible. Discuss this story with a friend or your parents. What were the motives of the people involved? What should they have done in place of the worldly wisdom they displayed? Was there a consequence to worldly wisdom in this story?

Recommended in: ◆ several lessons in this unit; ◗ several HOW unit studies. ◗■ Key Resource for this unit.

Do you realize how blessed you are? Your parents have made a decision about your education that may go against the grain in some geographical areas. Yet they have still chosen a road that will enable you to experience God-filled, Bible-based education as you are growing up.

Write your parents a letter thanking them for their decision. Tell them the reasons why you appreciate being homeschooled and how it is affecting your life for good.

Purpose in your heart to seek godly counsel and wisdom each day. Avoid the wisdom of the world. Pray and repent for any areas in which you've already made mistakes with the world's wisdom. Ask God to help you discern the difference between His wisdom and that of the world.

Benefits of Wisdom LS10103

Step 1: Excite

Think about and discuss how decisions you make during your teen years will affect you later in life (which school you might attend, the people you associate with, a job you might take, etc.).

Brainstorm and make a list of a dozen benefits of wisdom. Unlike many brainstorming activities, do not hurry with this one. Take at least ten minutes to really think about your answers.

After you've completed your list, decide which benefit is the most important one to you. Share this answer with a parent or friend. Why is this benefit important in your personal life? Are you experiencing this benefit in your life right now? If not, what kind of changes can you make that would produce this benefit in your life?

Step 2: Examine

J. E. Smith explains in *The Wisdom Literature and Psalms* that several promises of protection are offered to one who clings to wisdom.

> **First**, he will walk "securely," i.e., free from anxiety and danger (Pro. 1:33). In that path there would be no danger one would "dash" the foot, i.e., trip over something.

> **Second**, the practitioner of wisdom will lie down without fear. His sleep will be "sweet," i.e., undisturbed by worry and guilt (Pro. 3:23-24).

> **Third**, one who walks in wisdom's paths should have no fear of "sudden terror," i.e., unexpected calamity. He can fearlessly face "the destruction of the wicked." This could be taken to be (1) the devastation caused by wicked men when they persecute the righteous; or (2) the devastation which God eventually brings on the wicked.

> **Fourth**, throughout life the Lord is the believer's "confidence." Those who rely on God will have no feeling of helplessness. The Lord would keep that one's foot from being caught in the snares set by evildoers (Pro. 3:25-26).

The Bible Knowledge Commentary gives the following note on Proverbs chapter 2:

> Wisdom gives positive, health-inducing moral benefits. It keeps one from evil and contributes to holiness. Wisdom is a matter of the heart and of moral conduct, not just of intellectual attainment. This is made clear by the words upright and blameless (cf. v. 21), the just, and faithful ones (those who are loyal to God). Elsewhere in Proverbs the word for victory is translated "sound judgment" (3:21; 8:14; 18:1). In 2:7 it means success, the result of sound judgment. Like a shield (cf. Ps. 3:3) God protects those who by His wisdom are morally upright, those who are His (cf. Prov. 1:33). Moral living enables a person to be equitable with others, to do what is right and just and fair (cf. 1:3). "Fair" translates the same word rendered "upright" in 2:7. One's conduct is

---

Recommended in: ◆ several lessons in this unit; ● several HOW unit studies. ☞ Key Resource for this unit.

suggested by the synonyms walk . . . course . . . way, and path (vv. 7-9; cf. vv. 12-13, 15, 18-20).

A person who strives for wisdom (vv. 1-4) will find that it will enter his heart (v. 10). Obtaining wisdom requires diligence on man's part in pursuing God's will; yet wisdom is a gift from God (cf. v. 6). Having such knowledge from God gives inner joy or pleasure.

Look up these verses in Proverbs:

- ◆ 2:4–5: Grow in our knowledge and understanding of who God is.
- ◆ 4:11–12, 10:13, 3:21–23: Get clear guidance and direction about life.
- ◆ 4:5–7, 28:26: God's divine protection.
- ◆ 14:15–16: Protection from evil.
- ◆ 2:10–22: Protection in our relationships.
- ◆ 2:8–10: Protection from making serious mistakes.
- ◆ 24:5: Provides strength and power from God.
- ◆ 3:13–18: Peace, contentment, and happiness will characterize our life.
- ◆ 8:32–35, 19:8: Contributes to a good self-image. We can love our own soul because we have God's viewpoint about our value.
- ◆ 8:17–21: Prosperity. Two kinds of wealth: spiritual and material.
- ◆ 3:7–8, 9:8–11, 15:24: Good health and a long life. We can accomplish more, achieve more, and be more productive.

Suggested Resources

Below are more resources on the benefits of wisdom.

Walking Wisely ●— ◆
Chapter 3, "Eight Amazing, Wonderful Benefits of Wisdom" (1–12). You will be advised to read other chapters with upcoming lessons in this book.

Internet Sources

An Autobiographical Sketch
Lesson 8 in the series of Bible lectures on Proverbs.
http://www.livingbiblestudies.org/study/JT49/008.html

The Benefits of Wisdom
A sermon by Dr. Charles Stanley. You can listen to the audio version or watch the video at Intouch Ministries' Web site:

RealAudio
http://www.intouch.org/intouch/site.show_page?p_id=76101&p_id_from=77395&p_current_date=07%2F13%2F2000

RealVideo
http://www.intouch.org/intouch/site.show_page?p_id=76101&p_id_from=77395&p_current_date=07%2F14%2F2000

The Benefits of Wisdom
A Bible study and commentary on Proverbs 3:1, 2, 4, 6, 7, 21–26,33.
http://www.victoryword.100megspop2.com/sermons/wisdom_ben.html

Step 3: Expand

Choose and complete one or more of the following activities:

Activity 1: Copy Passages
Copy the Proverbs outline from Step 2 and the Bible verses into your portfolio. Spend some time meditating on one or two of these passages.

Activity 2: Outline
Outline Proverbs chapter 2. Refer to the outline example at http://HeartofWisdom.com/Worksheets.htm.

Activity 3: Apply the Word
Select one lesson you've learned from the Proverbs passages in Step 2 and apply it to your life. For example, if you select the passage about prosperity from Proverbs chapter 8, there is a condition or a requirement to receiving the benefit. The requirement in verse 17 is that you must love wisdom and diligently seek it to receive the listed benefits. How can you begin to apply this Scripture to your life? How can you diligently seek wisdom? How can you apply the Scripture that you selected? Write a one-page essay on what you are doing to apply God's Word in your own life. Keep a journal or a diary to record any benefits you notice in your life as the result of applying God's Word. Refer to http://HeartofWisdom.com/Writing.htm.

Activity 4: Write a Research Paper
Research biblical people who used wisdom, and the benefits that it brought in their lives. Use your Bible, Bible commentaries, Bible dictionaries, and other such reference tools. Chronicle the lives of at least three people in your paper. Be sure to include a bibliography and footnotes. Your paper should be a minimum of one page about each Bible character. Refer to http://HeartofWisdom.com/Writing.htm

Activity 5: Compare and Contrast
Using your Bible, compare and contrast the lives of two biblical people: one who made wise choices and another who was unwise. You may present your findings in one of two ways: an oral presentation or a two-page written report.

Activity 6: Prepare and Conduct an Interview
Choose an adult who you admire to interview. Prepare a list of questions (refer to "Preparing an Interview" in *Writers INC*) to ask about wise or unwise decisions that person made in his or her life. Include: What decisions did you make during your teen years that still affect you today?

Recommended in: ◆ several lessons in this unit; ● several HOW unit studies. ☞ Key Resource for this unit.

Activity 7: Compare and Contrast
In this activity, do not use people found in the Bible; rather compare and contrast two people in our world today. Choose one who you feel is wise, and another that seems to display a lack of wisdom. Your choices may include entertainment personalities, politicians, world leaders, and so on. Gather specific information about their choices and be detailed in why you see each as wise or unwise. Present your findings in a ten-minute oral presentation.

Step 4: Excel

Look back at step 1 and the brainstorming list you made. Determine to make life choices that will allow these benefits to operate in your life. What kinds of changes do you need to make? Where are you hitting the mark? Make a list of possible changes or enhancements you can make in your life that will allow these benefits to begin operating on your behalf. If you need help implementing life changes, consult your parents or your pastor.

Acquiring Wisdom LS10104

Step 1: Excite

Which do you think is more important: wisdom, knowledge, or intelligence? Explain your answer. How do you think a person can actually acquire wisdom? Is it genetic? Is it only for special people?

Wisdom is the capacity to view things from God's perspective and respond according to biblical principles. Wisdom has often been confused with knowledge or intelligence. But while wisdom may encompass those things, it is not limited by them.

Brainstorm and discuss the text above. Can you give at least one example of godly wisdom? Share your ideas about wisdom. As you study this unit, decide if your answers line up with what you learn.

Step 2: Examine

If wisdom is a path, Proverbs 2:1–9 is the map showing how to find the path.

> *My son, if thou wilt receive my words, and hide my commandments with thee; So that thou incline thine ear unto wisdom, and apply thine heart to understanding; Yea, if thou criest after knowledge, and liftest up thy voice for understanding; If thou seekest her as silver, and searchest for her as for hid treasures; Then shalt thou understand the fear of the LORD, and find the knowledge of God. For the LORD giveth wisdom: out of his mouth cometh knowledge and understanding. He layeth up sound wisdom for the righteous: he is a buckler to them that walk uprightly. He keepeth the paths of judgment, and preserveth the way of his saints. Then shalt thou understand righteousness, and judgment, and equity; yea, every good path.*

The Hebrew root word stating the basic concept of wisdom appears over 300 times in the Old Testament. It centers our attention on a person's basic approach to life and moral values. Wisdom is fundamentally the choice to be godly. The wise person is sensitive to God, obeys Him, and applies God's Word to choices in everyday life.

There are four basic steps to acquiring wisdom: (1) Fearing God (reverence), (2) Studying His Word, (3) Obedience, and (4) Prayer.

1. Fear of the Lord: The terms *the fear of the Lord* and *fear the Lord* occur fifteen times in Proverbs. Having the right reverence and attitude toward God is the first step taken toward wisdom's path. In the *New International Version* Bible the *fear of the Lord* is described as "loving reverence." In the *Amplified Bible* the *fear of the Lord* is described as "reverent and worshipful." A rabbinic commentary explains that *fear* here is not dread but "reverence of God expressed in submission to His will." The *Ryrie Study Bible* provides the term "a reverence for God expressed in submission to His will." Scofield notes that the *fear of the Lord* is a "reverential trust with hatred of evil." *The Full Life Bible* comments on *the fear of the Lord* as "A reverent awe of God's power, majesty, and holiness [which] produces in us a holy fear of transgressing His revealed will.

Recommended in: ◆ several lessons in this unit; ● several HOW unit studies. ◉▬ Key Resource for this unit.

We are not qualified to profit by the instructions that are given us unless our minds be possessed with a holy reverence of God, and every thought within us be brought into obedience to him (Matthew Henry 1991). Consequently, no intellectual pursuit is sound without the fear of the Lord. The acquirement of wisdom is not an "academic" pursuit but, essentially, a theological and spiritual activity. (Read Prov. 14:26,27; 19:23; 23:17–18, 10:27; Phil. 2:12; and Ps. 2:11.)

2. Study God's Word: Proverbs 1:5 says: *A wise man will hear, and will increase learning; and a man of understanding shall attain unto wise counsels.* Wise people listen to wise instruction, especially the Word of God. To acquire true wisdom we must diligently spend time carefully studying the Word of God. In Mark 4:24, Jesus tells us to pay attention to what we hear: "*And he said unto them, Take heed what ye hear: with what measure ye mete, it shall be measured to you: and unto you that hear shall more be given.*" In Luke 8:18, Jesus tells us to pay attention to how we hear, "*Take heed therefore how ye hear: for whosoever hath, to him shall be given; and whosoever hath not, from him shall be taken even that which he seemeth to have.*" Knowledge of Scripture is not enough: "*Knowledge puffs up, but love builds up*" (1 Cor. 8:1). You can pursue knowledge, but if you are off course it will all be in vain: "*Of making many books there is no end; and much study is a weariness of the flesh*" (Eccl. 12:12). Knowledge can be memorized. Wisdom means that you must think things through. Wisdom is the something that enables us to use knowledge rightly . . . *Wisdom.* You will learn more about studying God's Word in the next lesson.

3. Obey God's Word: A wise person is careful about what they read and about their radio and television selections. Wise people listen to wise counsel (Prov. 13:10; 12:15; 19:20) and profit from rebuke (Prov. 9:8–9; 10:17; 17:10). Wise people are careful about who they associate with; they resist group pressures and think for themselves. Wise people connect God's words and everyday experience, and it is only in the way a person lives his life that wisdom can be demonstrated. You will learn more about obedience in another lesson.

4. Pray for Wisdom: James 1:5 says: *If any of you lacks wisdom, he should ask God, who gives generously to all without finding fault, and it will be given to him.* Ask and receive. *If ye abide in* [Jesus], *and* [His] *words abide in you, ye shall ask what ye will, and it shall be done unto you* (John 15:7). You will learn more about praying for wisdom in another lesson.

Suggested Resources

Below are more resources about acquiring wisdom.

Walking Wisely ●— ◆
Chapter 4, "The Essentials for Walking in Wisdom" (67–110). Read this chapter in its entirety now and reread the sections suggested in the next lessons. You will be advised to read other chapters with upcoming lessons in this book.

Additional Reading

Be Skillful. An Old Testament Study by Warren Wiersbe
Wiersbe takes a look at the original "success manual," the Book of Proverbs, to show how you can choose the right path of life, deal with wrong choices, make the best use of your time and money, build a happy home life, and more. Includes a chapter on The Path of Wisdom and Life (Prov. chapters 2–4).

Internet Sources

Get Wisdom
Article on Proverbs 4:1–13 by a Baptist pastor, explaining that true wisdom will bring ultimate and eternal happiness.
http://www.soundofgrace.com/piper81/052481m.htm

Get Wisdom and Discernment
Article on wisdom by Nathan Mates.
http://www.visi.com/~nathan/xtian/wisdom.htm

How Much Better Is It to Get Wisdom Than Gold!
A list of Bible verses comparing wisdom with gold.
http://www.topical-bible-studies.org/06-0004.htm

How to Acquire Wisdom
A sermon by Dr. Charles Stanley in RealAudio format. Ultimate and eternal happiness is what wisdom will bring.
http://www.intouch.org/intouch/site.show_page?p_id=76101&p_id_from=77395&p_current_date=07%2F11%2F2000

How to Acquire Wisdom
A sermon by Dr. Charles Stanley in video format.
http://www.intouch.org/myintouch/broadcasts/tv_sermons_77546.html

Step 3: Expand

Complete Activity 1 and one other activity.

Activity 1: Write Summaries
Write a summary for each of the four basic steps to acquiring wisdom. You will be using these summaries for work in the next lessons.

1. **Seek wisdom with a fear of the Lord** (Prov. 1:7, 2:4, 8:17).
2. **Meditate upon His Word** (Prov. 2:1, 3:1, 4:20).
3. **Practice obedience** (Prov. 2:7, 8:33, 10:8).
4. **Pray for wisdom** (Prov. 11:2; Jas. 3:5–6).

Recommended in: ♦ several lessons in this unit; ♥ several HOW unit studies. ☀ Key Resource for this unit.

Activity 2: Copy Bible Passages
Copy the Bible verses listed in Activity 1 above and add them to your portfolio. Choose the verse that means the most to you. Share your thoughts about that one particular verse with a parent or friend.

Activity 3: Evaluate Your Life
Proverbs 4:7–9 says:

> *Wisdom is the principal thing; Therefore get wisdom. And in all your getting, get understanding. Exalt her, and she will promote you; She will bring you honor. She will place on your head an ornament of grace; A crown of glory, she will deliver to you.*

This passage of Scripture lists at least four benefits of getting wisdom. List the benefits you see in this passage and then honestly evaluate your life in light of these specific things. Are you experiencing these benefits in your life? If not, what can you do to get wisdom and enjoy the benefits of such in your life?

Activity 4: Write a Personal Essay
Can you think of an instance in which you made a really wise decision that paid off? How about a time that an unwise decision cost you a stiff consequence? Write a one-page essay about a personal experience in each of these areas. What did you do right? What could you have done better? Refer to http://HeartofWisdom.com/Writing.htm.

Activity 5: Study the Life of Solomon
Solomon is said to have been the wisest man who ever lived. Read the story of how he acquired wisdom in 1 Kings 3:1–15. After reading this passage, write down your understanding of how Solomon acquired wisdom. What else did God give him? Why did God give him other gifts? How can you apply the lesson of Solomon's story to your own life? Write down your ideas in your portfolio. Discuss with a parent or friend.

Activity 6: Pray
Wisdom comes from God.
James 1:5 tells us that if we lack wisdom, we can ask God for it and He will give it to us. Read and meditate on this verse of Scripture. Spend some time praying and asking God specifically about wisdom in your life. Be sure to block out at least thirty minutes of time when you can be alone with God. Write down anything that God speaks to your heart as you are praying.

Step 4: Excel

What have you learned about wisdom? Did you learn anything about God's perspective of wisdom? Share the most important or profound thing you learned in this lesson. Set specific goals regarding acquiring and applying wisdom in your own life. Work with a friend to stay accountable and attain the goals you have set. Let your friend be accountable to you as well.

Studying God's Word Wisely LS10105

Step 1: Excite

How long could you live without food? How well do you think your brain would function if you went several weeks without food? Would you be weak? Have you ever seen a hungry baby? A newborn can become very loud very quickly once he goes a few hours without milk.

God says that a Christian ought to have the same intense hunger for the Word of God that a baby has for milk, because God uses His Word to feed and nourish us so that we can be strong and grow.

> *As newborn babes, desire the sincere milk of the Word,*
> *that ye may grow thereby.* (1 Pet. 2:2)

Bible study is essential for spiritual growth. Psalm 19:10 says that the the Word of God is to be more desired than gold, more desired than much fine gold, and sweeter than honey and the honeycomb. God's Word is food to our spirits; when we miss a "meal" we become weak. Breakfast is said to be the most important meal of the day. The Bible provides us with the spiritual equivalent of good nutrition to get going with your day and to encourage us to live each day wisely and well. How often do you eat? How often do you read your Bible?

Step 2: Examine

You can always tell what holds importance in a person's life by the amount of time they put into different things. Athletes train long hours to reach the goals they have set. They have placed value on that specific area of their lives. What about musicians? To really utilize God-given musical talents, one must block out large amounts of time to spend practicing their instrument or their voice lessons. It is fine to put time and energy into things like music, sports, academics, and so on. As a matter of fact, it's an honorable thing if the motive and the goals are good and godly. However, we should always remember to put God first in everything. By putting God first, we will spend time praying, worshipping, and studying His Word.

It benefits every Christian to learn how to correctly interpret, understand, and apply the Bible. The Bible was written by people who lived and wrote in times and cultures vastly different from ours. To correctly interpret what the Bible says, we need to read it prayerfully and have Bible study tools on hand to help us understand the culture, history, and geography of the time it was written.

> *My son, if thou wilt receive my words, and hide my commandments with thee; So that thou incline thine*
> *ear unto wisdom, and apply thine heart to understanding.* (Prov. 2:1–2)

Recommended in: ◆ several lessons in this unit; ❤ several HOW unit studies. ●➞ Key Resource for this unit.

Bible study involves reading carefully, taking notes, and reflecting on the information. God promises that if we seek Him, He will speak to us through His Word and guide us in all our ways.

The word *hermeneutics* is from the Greek words *herme neuo*. It means "to interpret" and it is used to denote the study and statement of the principles on which a text—for our purposes, the biblical text—is to be understood. *Hermeneutics* includes all the rules, principles, theories, and methods of interpreting the Bible.

Exegesis is the application of hermeneutical principles to decide what a text says and means in its historical, theological, contextual, literary, and cultural setting. The meaning thus obtained will be in agreement with other related Scriptures (MacArthur 1997).

There are three basic steps to all Bible study: **Observation, Interpretation**, and **Application**.

    1. **Observation** answers the question, "What does the passage say?"
    2. **Interpretation** answers the question, "What does the passage mean?"
    3. **Application** answers the question, "How does this truth relate to me?"

Basic Bible Study Principles

1. The Historical Principle: Knowing the historical setting of a passage is a great help to understanding its meaning. The historical background of a passage often is the major key to its interpretation.

2. The Cultural Principle: The cultural setting in which the Bible was written is very different from our twentieth-century Western culture. To interpret each part properly, one must understand the culture of its time.

3. The Literal or Grammar Principle: This principle interprets Scripture by taking into consideration the context of a passage and the grammatical uses of the words. The literal method allows Scripture interpret Scripture. "Words are arranged in larger units or patterns of meaning ranging from phrases to sentences, paragraphs, chapters, and sections. To analyze these, it is often necessary to examine the grammar of a language..." (Achtemeier 1985)

4. The Context Principle: This principle interprets in the light of the setting, and looks at the passage in context of the surroundings of a portion of a word, or a group of words. A text without a context is a pretext. Precept must be upon precept, precept upon precept; line upon line, line upon line (Isa. 28:10). Several paragraphs preceding and following the passage should also be studied.

5. The Literary Principle: The literary mold in which the language is cast is often crucial to our interpretation (narratives, poetry, prophecy, letters, proverbs, drama, law, wisdom literature, apocalyptic literature, parables). The genre of the passage and how words are arranged make a difference to our understanding.

The Handbook to Bible Study explains:

In order to work with the Bible, to apply it in a living way, and to avoid confusion, it is essential to grasp its overall plan and general structure. The books of the Bible were written at various times by a spectrum of authors, each of whom took pen in hand for a different purpose. The Old Testament is a record of God's creative activity and subsequent work preparatory to providing salvation and blessing the human race through the descendants, and in particular one descendant of one man, Abraham. It is not, as some have claimed, an account of the awakenings and development of the religious consciousness of humanity, but rather a divinely revealed documentation of God's dealings with people in preparation for the appearance of the God-man, Jesus Christ. The New Testament is the record of that appearance in space and time, at the focal point of all history, and its subsequent impact during the first century. Every book of the sixty-six contributes in some way to these central features of biblical history. (Karleen, P. S. 1987)

Bible Study Approaches

The three steps we discussed earlier, **Observation, Interpretation, and Application,** are the basics of Bible study, now we will examine several different approaches utilizing this three-step method.

These were more noble than those in Thessalonica, in that they received the word with all readiness of mind, and searched the scriptures daily, whether those things were so. (Acts 17:11).

Bible study approaches fall into three groups: **panoramic, telescopic**, and **microscopic**.

The Panoramic View seeks to encompass the overall view of the Bible or a passage of scripture. The Heart of Wisdom approach on the next page begins pursuing a panoramic view of the whole Bible reading it through in a year in order to get the big picture.

The Telescopic View concentrates attention on one place at a time, so we can view the Bible such as a topical study, on one specific theme or word at a time.

The Microscopic View involves vocabulary and language study, as well as the examination of biblical history and culture.

Whatever Bible study approach works best for you is fine as long as you rely on God's Spirit to guide you. The most important thing for us to remember is not to focus upon the quantity of information we learn, but to remain faithful to whatever spiritual truth God has entrusted to our care. One of the most important resolutions that any Christian ever make is to daily study God's Word.

Whatever method you use begin your study with prayer; as the psalmist says, *Open my eyes, that I may behold wondrous things out of thy law.* (Ps. 119:18).

Pray as Paul prayed for the Ephesians, *...that the God of our Lord Jesus Christ, the Father of glory, may give you a spirit of wisdom and revelation in the knowledge of him, having the eyes of your hearts enlightened, that you may know...*(Eph. 1:17, 18).

Recommended in: ◆ several lessons in this unit; ● several HOW unit studies. ●━ Key Resource for this unit.

Heart of Wisdom Bible Study

The Heart of Wisdom's approach to Bible study is a simple method. As a family, you will use a chronological Bible reading plan daily, to read through the Bible each year. This will give you the whole picture, a panoramic view. The Bible reading plan is the foundation. You are encouraged follow the Holy Spirit's leading to branch off into in-depth historical, topical, or word studies using telescopic and microscopic methods.

The goals are:

1. For families to read though the entire Bible in order to gain a view of the whole picture of God's Word.

2. For family members to interact while studying together. Children of all ages benefit from their parents' wisdom. Also, parents learn with their children.

3. For parents and children to learn to use Bible study tools (Bible atlas, Bible dictionary, lexicons, chronology charts, concordance, etc.).

4. For each student to document what was learned, on his or her own level, through the creation of a portfolio (consisting of time lines, summary writing, copying Bible passages, essay writing, paraphrasing, coloring pages, puzzles, etc.). Each year, the student begins a new portfolio. This provides parents and their children the opportunity to look back through the portfolios and observe the spiritual growth over the years.

5. For families to study God's Word in the light of the ancient Hebraic culture. We study a Hebrew book—written by Hebrews; we serve a Hebrew Lord—who had Hebrew disciples; we desire to follow the first-century church—which was first predominately Hebrew; and through Christ, we are grafted into a Hebrew family tree. It makes sense to study the Hebraic culture.

The daily Bible readings are divided in such a way that the amount of daily reading time is approximately the same each week. There is nothing special about the one-year (or 52-week) time frame. You can learn just as effectively by reading though the Bible in two years or longer. This program is simply a framework.

For more on Heart of Wisdom methods see:

The Heart of Wisdom Teaching Approach
A book to help homeschoolers make the Bible the focus of their teaching.

The Heart of Wisdom Teaching Approach
Includes an overview of the Heart of Wisdom Bible study approach and Bible reading plan. http://homeschoolunitstudies.com/Bible.htm

Inductive Bible Study

The inductive Bible study method entails the use of inductive reasoning to study the Bible. It consists of the observation of evidence, examination of the evidence, and a conclusion based upon that evidence. Inductive goes from specific to general. The learner examines the text, takes notes, and draws a conclusion.

The inductive Bible study method is explained in detail in *How to Study Your Bible* by Kay Arthur. Arthur suggests using colored pencils or markers to mark passages with colors and symbols as you read through the Bible. By looking at the Bible pages with colors, symbols, and groups (lists), students can immediately gain insight into what God is teaching. The reader will be able to graphically visualize the relationships within God's Word. Inductive Bible-study techniques can be used for word, topic, and/or people studies.

First, read slowly through the passage without any explanatory notes or other help. Ask questions designed to sharpen your observations. Note words or expressions which keep recurring, or which correspond or contrast. Observe people or things involved in the action, what they do, what they say, and what happens to them. Notice places and movements. Are certain places connected to a particular person or idea? Look at the indicators of time such as indicators of time such as verb tenses. Make notations with colored pencils, such as yellow for the name of Jesus, green for promises, and orange for salvation, or use symbols such as a triangle for trinity, heart for love, etc. Make notes in the margins such as:

- Who the passage was written by and to

- Key words and phrases

- Conclusions

For more on the inductive method see:

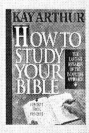

How to Study Your Bible by Kay Arthur
A dynamic guide to cultivating step-by-step Bible study skills such as observation, interpretation, application, and more—skills that mean the difference between being a passive spectator and an active participant in God's Word! Paperback - 176 pages (March 1994). Harvest House Publishers, Inc.; ISBN: 1565071735.

The New Inductive Study Bible by Kay Arthur
I use *The Narrated Bible* to read aloud with my children and *The New Indectutive Bible* for my personal studies. Inductively explore for yourself what God's Word has to say about your life, instead of just what the "experts" say. With wide margins for note-taking and individually designed charts for each book, *The New Inductive Study Bible* is a systematic, effective way to discover the treasures of God's Word. Hardcover, 2,240 pages (2000). Harvest House Publishers; ISBN: 0736900160. E-mail info@heartofwisdom.com to request a sample booklet with a detailed description of this Bible. Place "Inductive Study Bible" in the subject line.

Precept Ministries International
Kay Arthur's Web site offers materials which allow students of all ages to observe, interpret, and apply the Bible in a fun and exciting way.
http://www.precept.org/

Recommended in: ◆ several lessons in this unit; ● several HOW unit studies. ●— Key Resource for this unit.

Book of The Bible Studies

You should not begin your study of a Bible book until you have read and observed the message and flow through all of it. Read the entire book several times during a month. Observe main themes, repeated words, main characters, and principal divisions. By the end of the month you will have a fairly good understanding of the book. Make an outline as you read. Answer the following:

(1) Author: Who is the author of the book? To whom is the author writing? What are the major personalities mentioned? How well do they know and understand each other?

(2) Historical Setting: When was the book written? What is the historical setting of the author? What is the historical setting of the recipients? What was happening in this part of the world at the time?

(3) Purpose: Why was the book written? If there was a problem to correct, what was it? What was the author trying to accomplish?

(4) Themes: What is the major emphasis of the book? What are some of the recurring ideas? What subjects does the book deal with?

Character Studies

First, choose a person in the Bible to study. Then, use a concordance to look up every place the person occurs. Pay attention to the character's growth in his or her relationship to God. What were the major events in his or her life? Who were some of his or her contemporaries? What was this character's major achievement; what influence did he or she have on people or events? Choose a summary Bible verse and a key verse that you feel best describe the character. Make a summary of the passage that you have read. Find out what the leading lesson is in this character's life. Identify problems or situations you have in common with the character. Consider making a time line of important events in the person's life.

Topical Studies

In the topical method, you select a topic such as "wisdom" and focus your Bible study on that topic using a Bible concordance or a topical Bible. First, determine the definition of the word (topic) that you want to study. Use a dictionary or use the Greek or Hebrew dictionary in the *Strong's Concordance*. Use your concordance to find the Scripture references for the word. Review these references and select the ones that are applicable to what you are studying. Review the actual Scriptures that you have selected from the concordance reference and be sure to review any other references that appear if you have a reference Bible. After you have gathered all of the information from the Scriptures, meditate on them and form a conclusion based on your findings.

Word Studies

Defining a word means conducting an investigation of what it may mean and what it does not mean. A word means what it means depending on when the author uses it. A single word may have different connotations in different passages. You need to be familiar with word studies because people can use a word study to make the Bible say something it does not say. Word studies must always be based on the original language, not solely on the English text. The context must verify the precise meaning of the word.

1. Select a word to study.

2. Look up the word in a concordance and find all the listings in a KJV.

3. Look up the number in *Strong's Exhaustive Concordance* to locate any other passages in which the English word is used by the same Bible author.

4. Look up the word in a Bible dictionary (such as *Vine's Complete Expository Dictionary of Old and New Testament Words*).

5. Compare various English versions to see how different translators used the word.

6. Define the English word using an English dictionary (preferably *Webster's 1828 version*).

7. Use a *lexicon* to look up the word in its original language. (http://crosswalk.com)

8. Trace the origin of the word.

9. Use Bible study tools to find any commentary on the word.

There are several computer software programs that make word studies very easy.

For more on word studies see:

The Complete Word Study New Testament by Spiros Zodhiates
Now you can dig into the original language of the New Testament without becoming a Greek scholar! This enriching resource assigns a Strong's reference number to every word in the KJV text, provides grammatical information about each word, and parses each verb. Includes a Greek concordance. Hardcover - 1334 pages (1991). AMG Publishers; ISBN: 0899576516.

The Complete Word Study Old Testament by Spiros Zodhiates
Studying Hebrew and Aramaic now takes one book, not your entire desktop! Every word in this Old Testament has its Strong's number and a grammatical code printed above the English text. *Strong's Dictionary of the Hebrew Bible,* which gives detailed definitions of key words, is included in the Study Helps section. Other helps include grammatical notations which explain the codes, and a translational reference index which links each English word of the KJV to all the Hebrew words it represents. Hardcover - 2609 pages (1994) AMG Publishers; ISBN: 0899576656.

Recommended in: ◆ several lessons in this unit; ● several HOW unit studies. ●— Key Resource for this unit.

Bible Study Tools

Bible Atlas

A good Bible atlas contains the following:
1. Maps that show the location of places, groups of people, and nations in the Bible.
2. Maps that illustrate specific historical events, such as the conquest of Canaan.
3. Geographical information about the various regions of Israel and Jordan, as well as Egypt and Mesopotamia.
4. Information about climate and weather, travel and roads.
5. A section on historical geography—an historical survey of the Bible that shows where and how geography played a role in the history of Bible times.
6. An index of biblical places.

We recommended the *Holman Bible Atlas* ❤ for older students (7th grade and up). It contains a wealth of information that accompanies the visually appealing, full-color maps, charts, and diagrams.

For younger grades we recommend *The Victor Journey through the Bible* and/or *Nelson's Illustrated Encyclopedia of the Bible*. Both books include maps and culture information in colorful visual illustrations. See detailed descriptions in the next pages.

Various Chronology Charts

You know the saying, "A picture is worth a thousand words." One of the most helpful ways to learn about Bible chronology is to examine certain chronology charts which have been especially prepared for the Bible student. Another way is to make your own Time Line Book (see instructions at http://Heartofwisdom.com) using the chronology charts for reference. Students will understand the Bible better by seeing everything in chronological order and will be able to learn when key people lived and when key events happened.

We recommend *Reproducible Maps, Charts, Time Lines and Illustrations* ❤ or *Chronological and Background Charts of the Old Testament,* and *Chronological and Background Charts of the New Testament.*

From *Reproducible Maps, Charts, Time Lines and Illustrations.*

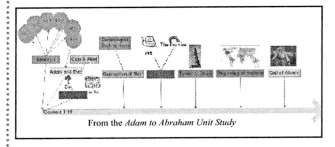

From the *Adam to Abraham Unit Study*

An Exhaustive Concordance

A concordance is an alphabetical list of all the words in the Bible. This is a helpful tool to have alongside your study Bible. Some Bibles have a limited concordance in the back, listing main words and names. An exhaustive concordance catalogues each usage of every word in the Bible, and lists each place that the word may be found.

We recommend *Strong's Exhaustive Concordance* or *Young's Analytical Concordance to the Bible.*

A Topical Bible

A topical Bible is similar to a concordance, except that it categorizes Bible verses by topic rather than by words. This is helpful because different verses dealing with the same topic or idea might not use the exact same words. The most widely used topical Bible is *Nave's Topical Bible*. It is available online: http://bible.crosswalk.com/

A Bible Dictionary and/or Bible Encyclopedia

A Bible dictionary explains many topics, words, customs, etc., found in the Bible. Bible dictionaries often include brief historical, archaeological, cultural, and geographical information.

A Bible encyclopedia is an expanded Bible dictionary with longer articles. These articles give more information and details than can be found in a Bible dictionary. We recommend *Nelson's Illustrated Encyclopedia of the Bible*, *New Bible Dictionary*, *The Eerdmans Bible Dictionary*, and *The Zondervan Pictorial Encyclopedia of the Bible*.

Nelson's Illustrated Encyclopedia of the Bible ●
provides an overview of significant turning points
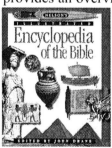
in biblical history, with maps, time lines, and special features about key people and places. A Peoples and Empires section offers intriguing insights on the nations that influenced the culture of the Jews and early Christians. It also contains a detailed study of the life, ministry, and message of Jesus plus a comprehensive survey of life in Bible times, including family life, social customs, and religious beliefs and practices from Abraham to the early church. Contemporary graphics visually enhance the biblical and historical images, making this the most complete, accurate, and eye-appealing Bible encyclopedia. Note: I disagree with a few paragraphs but thats not bad out of 330 pages.

Commentaries

Commentaries are collections of explanations, notes, and interpretations of the text of a particular book or section of the Bible. When used properly, they can greatly help you in your Bible studies. Remember that commentaries are written by men who can be, and often are, fallible. *Never* let reading any man's writing become a substitute for reading God's Word.

My favorite commentary is the *Teacher's Commentary* by Lawrence Richards. It is specifically designed for teachers. I refer to to several times a week. It features a "Link to Life" teaching ideas on three age levels: children, youth and adult. Includes a leader's teaching plan for all ages.

My favorite Bible study tool for my children is *The Victor Journey Through the Bible* ●. It's like a commentary/atlas/Bible handbook. It is a unique resource that approaches the Bible story by story which is perfect to use while reading through the Bible chronologically. In these pages you will discover around 250 of your favorite Bible stories presented with background

information in words and pictures. Includes these features:

- over 400 colorful pages of photographs, drawings, maps, and charts,
- more than 100 drawings from objects or monuments of Bible times,
- over 200 photographs of Bible lands today,
- photographs of more than 50 archaeological discoveries,
- scores of reconstructions and diagrams,
- and dozens of colorful maps.

Recommended in: ◆ several lessons in this unit; ● several HOW unit studies. ●— Key Resource for this unit.

This book explains how ancient people really lived-the foods they ate, the homes they lived in, the clothes they wore, the work they performed. Every home should have this complete reference work on its shelves. It will enrich lesson preparation, Bible storytelling, family devotions, and Bible study.

Word Studies

Word studies allow you to study the original Hebrew and/or Greek words from the Bible without knowing either language. A good set of word studies will tell you the original root meaning of the Greek or Hebrew word, the different ways in which that particular word is used both in the Bible and in secular writings of the same time, and how often and where the word is used in Scripture. They range from inexpensive single volumes to expensive multi-volume sets.

We recommend *The Word Study Concordance* and *The Complete Word Study New Testament*, *Vine's Complete Expository Dictionary of Old and New Testament Words*, *Wilson's Old Testament Word Studies*, *Wuest's Word Studies in the Greek New Testament*, and *Vincent's Word Studies of the New Testament*.

Crosswalk.com provides online lexicons. You simply type in the Strong's Concordance number or English word, to find the Greek or Hebrew words and meanings.
http://bible.crosswalk.com/Lexicons/

Books About Bible Study

Living by the Book by Howard Hendricks
This is an excellent book on basic biblical interpretation. How would you describe your personal Bible study? Mundane or motivational? Lackluster or lively? Redundant or reviving? Includes extensive chapters on: observation (how to read, things to look for); interpretation (content, context, comparison, culture, figurative language, etc.); application (life change, principles, etc.). Foreword by Chuck Swindoll. Paperback - 349 pages (1993). Moody Press; ISBN: 0802408168.

30 Days to Understanding the Bible (Expanded Edition) by Max E. Anders
If you are new to the Bible and want to get a good overview quickly this book is you! Full of great tips and symbols to help adults or children remember the chronological order of events and books. This is an outstanding resource that has brought the Bible's message home to thousands—in just one month! Featuring thirty easy-to-follow, fifteen-minute lessons, it offers an overview of the Bible and covers every major era of biblical history. A twelve-week teaching plan, makes this ideal for homeschoolers. Paperback - 248 pages (1994). Word Publishing; ISBN: 084993575X.

Get Organized!

Keep all Bible study tools, pencils, etc., on a specific shelf, or in a crate or basket near your designated study area. Don't be interrupted by having to stop and look for a reference book in the middle of a reading. You should have a study Bible with wide margins for writing notes, lists, comparisons, etc. If you don't have such a Bible, use a spiral notebook for Bible note-taking. Be diligent about your study time and maintaining your Bible study tools and notebook.

Bible Study Tools On the Internet

ⓘ *Basic Bible Study Tools*
A list of the fundamental Bible study tools on the Heart of Wisdom Web site.
http://homeschoolunitstudies.com/Bible/bibletools.htm

ⓘ *Basics of the Bible*
A Web site to help those who want to learn about Bible interpretation. It covers the basic rules and guidelines of interpretation.
http://www.bible-interpretation.com/

ⓘ *Bible Study Introduction*
The Building Bible School (BBS) System helps build your knowledge of God and the Bible. Not associated directly with any denomination, sect, division, or church.
http://www.bible-study-free.org/

ⓘ *Bible Study Gateway*
A free service for reading and researching Scripture online-- all in the language or translation of your choice! They provide advanced searching capabilities based on keywords or scripture references, and various other tools to enhance your study of the Bible.
http://www.biblegateway.com/

ⓘ *Bible Study Tools*
Use these award-winning Bible search engine and study tools to deepen your walk with God. Here you will find searchable Bibles (several versions), Bible dictionaries, concordances, lexicons (Greek and Hebrew word study tools), Bible encyclopedias, concordances, and more. http://bible.crosswalk.com/

ⓘ *Learning to Use My Bible*
A fun hangman interactive game based on Bible study (several puzzles available).
http://www.quia.com/servlets/quia.activities.common.ActivityPlayer?AP_rand=1770864554&AP_activityType=8&AP_urlId=19649&AP_continuePlay=true&id=19649

ⓘ *Online Bible Study*
This site is designed to improve your knowledge of the Bible. The Bible study maps will help you better understand the places mentioned in the Bible, and the crossword puzzles will make your online Bible study an enjoyable spiritual exercise.
http://jesusanswers.com/bible/study.htm

ⓘ The Bible Online
The bible online; bible courses, bible study, devotionals and answers.
http://www.bible.com/

ⓘ StudyLight.org
Bible study resources to deepen your walk with God. http://www.studylight.org/

Recommended in: ◆ several lessons in this unit; ♥ several HOW unit studies. ☞ Key Resource for this unit.

Bible study methodologies and techniques are fruitless unless we are dependent on God's Spirit for illumination of his Word to our minds and hearts.

Step 3: Expand

Choose and complete at least three of the activities below.

Activity 1: Write an Essay
In the last lesson you should have completed Activity 1, writing summary paragraphs for each of the four basic steps to acquiring wisdom. Use what you have learned in this lesson to expand the summary paragraph you wrote about "Studying God's Word" into an essay on this topic. Refer to http://HeartofWisdom.com/Writing.htm.

Activity 2: Complete a Bible Study
Study 1 Corinthians 1:19–27 using the following study method outlined in *The Teachers Commentary:*

1. Read and reread a section to determine its subject
2. Make a one-sentence summary of each paragraph within the section
3. Rework sentences into a brief paraphrase of the section
4. Go back and examine each paragraph in the text in more detail
5. Determine and apply major teachings (principles)

Activity 3: Do a Word Study
Do a word study on *study*.

1. Identify the Strong's number assigned to the word *study*.
2. Determine the basic meaning of the word.
3. See how this word is used elsewhere in the book you are studying.

Present your findings in a one-page written report that is to be presented orally to your parents, friends, or homeschooling group.

Activity 4: Complete an Inductive Bible Study
Study the Gospel of John using the inductive Bible study method.

Activity 5: Write a Paper
Apply study in your life. Choose one section of Scripture that you will study over a one-month period. For example, you may choose one of the Gospels, or a section of Proverbs. Whatever you select, study that portion of Scripture systematically every day for an entire month. Use study aids if necessary. Record your findings each day and be sure to include anything that you feel the Lord is speaking to you during this time of intense, specific study. Write a five-page paper at the conclusion of the month, explaining what you learned from this portion of the Bible. Include personal insights if desired. This paper should be grammatically correct, with any necessary footnotes or bibliography included.

Activity 6: Create an Outline
Outline a book of the Bible. Here is an example of how to begin the Gospel of Matthew:

I. Introduction to the Messiah (1:1–4:11)
    A. The Jewish Lineage of Christ (1:1–17)
    B. Messiah's Birth and Escape to Egypt (1:18–2:23)
    C. John the Baptist Prepares the Way for the Messiah (3:1–12)
    D. Baptism of the Messiah (3:13–17)
    E. Temptation of the Messiah (4:1–12)

II. Jesus' Ministry in and Near Galilee (4:12–18:35)
    A. Early Ministry in Galilee (4:12–25)
    B. Discussion about Discipleship in the Kingdom (5:1–7:29)

Activity 7: Do Research
Gather Bible study tools: a study Bible, a Bible dictionary, a Bible handbook, a concordance, a Bible manners and customs book, and a topical Bible. Join a friend to have a "study marathon." Pick a biblical person, word, or topic prior to your session that both you and your friend agree on. Give yourselves one hour to find as much information as possible on the topic you've selected. Arrange your findings in a list and have the other person do the same. Compare your information on the subject. How many pieces of information were found by each of you? Who found the most information? Who found the most unique or interesting piece of information? Compare your findings and share information with one another. Do you feel that you utilized good study skills to discover information on your subject? Could you now study the information you've gathered and become knowledgeable on the subject? Share your thoughts.

Activity 8: Outline
Read and outline the article "Study is a Form of Worship" by Dr. John Garr.
http://heartofwisdom.com/newsletter/V1/article6507.htm

Activity 9: Copy Bible Passages
Copy all the verses below and add them to your Portfolio.

- **2 Tim. 2:15**—*Study to shew thyself approved unto God, a workman that needeth not to be ashamed, rightly dividing the word of truth.*

- **Acts 17:11**—*These were more noble than those in Thessalonica, in that they received the word with all readiness of mind, and searched the scriptures daily, whether those things were so.*

- **1 Pet. 3:15**—*But sanctify the Lord God in your hearts: and be ready always to give an answer to every man that asketh you a reason of the hope that is in you with meekness and fear.*

- **Jude 3**—*Beloved, when I gave all diligence to write unto you of the common salvation, it was needful for me to write unto you, and exhort you that ye should earnestly contend for the faith which was once delivered unto the saints.*

- **1 Thes. 5:21**—*Prove all things; hold fast that which is good.*

Recommended in: ♦ several lessons in this unit; ● several HOW unit studies. ●━ Key Resource for this unit.

- **2 Tim. 3:14–17**—*But continue thou in the things which thou hast learned and hast been assured of, knowing of whom thou hast learned them; And that from a child thou hast known the holy scriptures, which are able to make thee wise unto salvation through faith which is in Christ Jesus. All scripture is given by inspiration of God, and is profitable for doctrine, for reproof, for correction, for instruction in righteousness: That the man of God may be perfect, thoroughly furnished unto all good works.*

- **Tit. 2:1**—*But speak thou the things which become sound doctrine: . . .*

- **Tit. 2:7**—*In all things shewing thyself a pattern of good works: in doctrine shewing uncorruptness, gravity, sincerity, . . .*

Step 4: Excel

Answer these questions to yourself:

- How much time each day do you set aside consistently for the study of God's Word?
- Do you spend enough time studying His Word?
- What can you do to change poor study habits?
- Do you have the necessary Bible study tools available?

Determine to become a person of study. Make the decision today to *study to show yourself approved unto God.* Memorize 2 Tim. 2:15 and then apply it to your life.

- Buy a three-ring notebook that can be used exclusively for notes to write down your thoughts while studying God's Word
- Select a quiet place where you can study
- Select a time for Bible study. Set aside an amount of time to study each day. Be flexible to God's leading
- Pray before each study

Choose one of the activities that you completed and present your findings to your family or homeschool group. Share your personal insights into the importance of godly study and how this lesson has impacted your life.

Obeying God's Word LS10106

Step 1: Excite

True wisdom begins when man humbles himself before God in reverence and worship and is obedient to His commands. Faithfulness to God requires being constantly determined to obey Him. When we choose to obey God, we choose the way of wisdom.

Why do you think the Bible says *to obey is better than sacrifice* (1 Sam. 15:22)? Why is obedience wise? Is disobedience foolishness (Matt. 7:24–27)? Is sin the spirit of lawlessness? Is disobedience the rejection of God's divine purpose?

Discuss a time when you were disobedient to your parents. What was the outcome of the situation? What would the outcome have been if you had been obedient?

Step 2: Examine

Harper's Bible Dictionary describes obedience as "submitting to the will or authority of another." The Old Testament has no separate word meaning "obey." *Obey* translates in the Hebrew "to hear" (Gen. 22:18; Isa. 42:24). The concept is also expressed as "keeping" or "observing" the commandments (Ex. 16:28; 34:11) and "walking" in God's ways (1 Kings 11:33). In the New Testament, Christ demonstrates His obedience to God (Rom. 5:19; Phil. 2:8; Heb. 5:8), and Christians are called to obedience of faith (Rom. 1:5; 16:26), obedience to Christ (John 3:36; Heb. 5:9), and obedience to the gospel (Rom. 10:16; 1 Pet. 4:17).

Jesus said, *"If ye love me, keep my commandments"* (John 14:15). His disciples are expected to follow the Bible commands. The Bible that Jesus and Paul used was what we now call the Old Testament. Jesus and Paul referred to the Old Testament consistently. When the words were written, *All scripture is inspired by God and is useful for teaching, for reproof, for correction, and for training in righteousness* (1 Tim. 3:16), they referred to what we call the Old Testament and what was then known as "Scripture." The commands or "law" they referred to was not a legal system; "law" was all-encompassing, full of God's mercy and grace. The Bible tells us that the law makes one wise.

> *The law of the LORD is perfect, converting the soul:*
> *the testimony of the LORD is sure, making wise the simple.* (Ps. 19:7)

The word *Law* in the Bible actually refers to something to teach or instruct believers how to live in ethical and moral harmony with their fellow man and before God. Roy Blizzard explains the etymology of the word *Law*: "The English word *law* is used to translate the Hebrew word *Torah*. Torah is the feminine noun from the root *yarah*. The root *yarah* means to throw, or to shoot, or to cast, as in the casting of lots, or the shooting of arrows. It means to point out, to show. It means to direct, to teach, to instruct. A moreh, in Hebrew, is a teacher, or one who throws out, or points out; one who directs or instructs. Torah is direction, or instruction. It sets forth the way man is to live. It instructs man as to how he is to live in an ethical and moral way among his fellow man and before God. . . . The idea of law in Hebrew is not something that, if transgressed, is going to get you *zapped*. Torah is instruction that, if followed, will enrich one's life; if ignored, will diminish it."

Recommended in: ◆ several lessons in this unit; ❤ several HOW unit studies. ●━ Key Resource for this unit.

Unfortunately, it has been difficult for both the Christian and the Jew to understand many of Paul's statements about law because of what others have said Paul was saying. Many Jewish theologians have written negatively about Paul and his teachings, based not upon a careful examination of Paul, but based upon what Christian theologians said about Paul. In Paul's day the *Tenak*, which was the Law, the prophets, and the Old Testament writings, were all the Scriptural text that was available. Both Jesus and Paul taught that believers should be guided by the Spirit of God to fulfill the Law through faith and love. Although Jesus fulfilled the ceremonial or sacrificial part of the Law by dying on the cross, we still see the principles of the Law, such as the priesthood and the atonement, evidenced today in the ministry of the church. In short, the manifestation has changed, but the spirit of the Law that exposes sin and produces light and life is the center of New Testament teaching. (Mosley 1995)

Read "The Nine-Fold Purpose of the Law" from *The Spirit of the Law* by Dr. Ron Mosley, below:

First - To teach the believer how to serve, worship, and please God [Psalm 19:7-9; Acts 18:13,14].
Second - To instruct the believer how to treat his fellow man and have healthy relationships with him [Leviticus 19:18; Galatians 5:14; Galatians 6:2].
Third: to teach believers how to be happy and prosper here on earth by manifesting the power and authority of God's reign in their lives [Joshua 1:8; Psalm 1:1-3; Luke 12:32].
Fourth - The Law was given, not to save, but to measure man's deeds toward both God and his fellow man, straightening out all matters contrary to sound doctrine [I Timothy 1:8-10; II Timothy 2:5; I Corinthians 6:1-12; I Corinthians 3:13; Romans 2:12; Revelation 20:12,13].
Fifth - The Law is a schoolmaster showing that we are guilty and then leading us to Christ, our Messianic justification [Galatians 3:21-24; Romans 3:19].
Sixth - The Law reveals to us both the knowledge and depth of our sin
[Romans 3:20; Romans 4:15; Romans 7:7,8; Luke 20:47 - greater damnation].
Seventh - The Law reveals the good, holy, just, and perfect nature of God and serves as the visible standard for God's will [Romans 2:17, and please God; Psalm 19:7-9; Acts 18:13,18; Romans 7:12; II Peter 1:4].
Eighth - The Law is to be established or accomplished by our faith, therefore, it is called the Law of faith [Romans 3:27; Romans 3:31].
Ninth - The same Law today is written on our hearts, and through God's Spirit, we can delight and serve the Law of God [Romans 7:6-25].

In Matt. 22:37–40 Jesus sums up the law in two commands quoted from Deut. 6:5 and Lev. 19:18:

Jesus said unto him,
Thou shalt love the Lord thy God with all thy heart,
and with all thy soul, and with all thy mind.
This is the first and great commandment.
And the second is like unto it,
Thou shalt love thy neighbour as thyself.
On these two commandments hang all the law and the prophets.

Love is the fullness of the Torah—not by superseding it, but through being the beginning, the end and the motivating force at work in it (Stern 1992). Scriptures say that the proof of God's presence within our lives is our willingness to share His love with others. Jesus said, *"All men will know that you are My disciples if you love one another"* (John 13:35).

A life of love is a deliberate choice. Love in action speaks louder than words. It is easy to say "I love God," but more difficult to choose to obey Him and turn away from our natural bent of self-centeredness. Obedience is critical in every area of our lives, but our obedience to God is an indication of whether or not we will be obedient in other areas of our lives. Practicing obedience in the little things can help us obey in critical issues. A child who is obedient to God will not have difficulty obeying his parents. An adult who lives a life of submission and obedience to God will not have a problem obeying his boss and getting to work on time. When we live a lifestyle of obedience, it becomes easy for God to impart His wisdom to us.

God is faithful to his obedient children. F. B. Meyer writes about Abraham's obedience: "There is nothing that God will not do for a man who dares to step out upon what seems to be the mist; who then finds rock beneath him as he puts his foot down."

Christians are helped to see discipleship's link between true faith and necessary obedience. Christians have often debated the relationship. But we can agree on certain basic statements. Salvation comes through faith and faith alone, for the death of Jesus purchased our forgiveness and new life. When a person has new life from God, that life will be expressed. Just as a living infant cries and moves, so a person with new life from Christ will express that life—in works. It is not that works bring life, but that those who are alive in Christ will work (Richards 1987). The Grace of God is what saves, not the law. But without the law we would not know what sin is. Paul said we are slaves to the law of God and to the law of sin. But we have been freed by the grace of God. The law shows us the way, the grace of God saves. The grace of God is not a new thing in the NT. The grace of God saved Noah and his family from the flood and Moses and the Hebrews from Egypt. Without God's instruction (commandments), how would we know what it was that God wanted us to do? The law shows us how we are to live.

Christ himself set the perfect illustration of obedience to the Father's will. Jesus was tempted just as we are; He was subject to weakness. He learned obedience through suffering. He was made perfect by His suffering. *Though he were a Son, yet learned he obedience by the things which he suffered; and being made perfect, he became the author of eternal salvation unto all them that obey him* (Heb. 5:8,9). Christ said, *"I came down from heaven, not to do mine own will, but the will of him that sent me"* (John 6:38). Christ also said, *"Not every one that saith unto me, Lord, Lord, shall enter into the kingdom of heaven; but he that doeth the will of my father which is in heaven"* (Matt. 7:21).

Read and discuss the following verses:

For this is the covenant that I will make with the house of Israel after those days, saith the Lord; I will put my laws into their mind, and write them in their hearts: and I will be to them a God, and they shall be to me a people. (Heb. 8:10–11)

For verily I say unto you, Till heaven and earth pass, one jot or one tittle shall in no wise pass from the law, till all be fulfilled. (Matt. 5:18)

Recommended in: ◆ several lessons in this unit; ♥ several HOW unit studies. ☛ Key Resource for this unit.

The statutes of the LORD are right, rejoicing the heart: the commandment of the LORD is pure, enlightening the eyes. (Ps. 19:8)

Wherefore the law is holy, and the commandment holy, and just, and good. (Rom. 7:12)

The law of the LORD is perfect, converting the soul: the testimony of the LORD is sure, making wise the simple. (Ps. 19:7)

Thy righteousness is an everlasting righteousness, and thy law is the truth. (Ps. 119:142)

For this is the love of God, that we keep his commandments: and his commandments are not grievous. (1 John 5:3)

But this thing commanded I them, saying, Obey my voice, and I will be your God, and ye shall be my people: and walk ye in all the ways that I have commanded you, that it may be well unto you. (Jer. 7:23)

A blessing, if ye obey the commandments of the LORD your God, which I command you this day: (Deut. 11:27)

Let us hear the conclusion of the whole matter: Fear God, and keep his commandments: for this is the whole duty of man. (Eccl. 12:13)

Let every soul be subject unto the higher powers. For there is no power but of God: the powers that be are ordained of God. (Rom. 13:1)

Ye shall walk after the LORD your God, and fear him, and keep his commandments, and obey his voice, and ye shall serve him, and cleave unto him. (Deut. 13:4)

For whosoever shall keep the whole law, and yet offend in one point, he is guilty of all. (Jas. 2:10)

Owe no man any thing, but to love one another: for he that loveth another hath fulfilled the law. (Rom. 13:8)

Love worketh no ill to his neighbour: therefore love is the fulfilling of the law. (Rom. 13:10)

He layeth up sound wisdom for the righteous: he is a buckler to them that walk uprightly. (Prov. 2:7)

The wise in heart will receive commandments: but a prating fool shall fall. (Prov. 10:8)

See, I have set before thee this day life and good, and death and evil; In that I command thee this day to love the LORD thy God, to walk in his ways, and to keep his commandments and his statutes and his judgments, that thou mayest live and multiply: and the LORD thy God shall bless thee in the land whither thou goest to possess it. (Deut. 30:15–16)

And thou shalt do that which is right and good in the sight of the LORD: that it may be well with thee, and that thou mayest go in and possess the good land which the LORD sware unto thy fathers. (Deut. 6:18)

Hear therefore, O Israel, and observe to do it; that it may be well with thee, and that ye may increase mightily, as the LORD God of thy fathers hath promised thee, in the land that floweth with milk and honey. (Deut. 6:3)

Wherefore it shall come to pass, if ye hearken to these judgments, and keep, and do them, that the LORD thy God shall keep unto thee the covenant and the mercy which he sware unto thy fathers: (Deut. 7:12)
O that there were such an heart in them, that they would fear me, and keep all my commandments always, that it might be well with them, and with their children for ever! (Deut. 5:29)

Keep therefore the words of this covenant, and do them, that ye may prosper in all that ye do. (Deut. 29:9)

Those things, which ye have both learned, and received, and heard, and seen in me, do: and the God of peace shall be with you. (Phil. 4:9)

Whosoever therefore shall break one of these least commandments, and shall teach men so, he shall be called the least in the kingdom of heaven: but whosoever shall do and teach them, the same shall be called great in the kingdom of heaven. (Matt. 5:19)

Therefore whosoever heareth these sayings of mine, and doeth them, I will liken him unto a wise man, which built his house upon a rock: And the rain descended, and the floods came, and the winds blew, and beat upon that house; and it fell not: for it was founded upon a rock. (Matt. 7:24–25)

If ye keep my commandments, ye shall abide in my love; even as I have kept my Father's commandments, and abide in his love. (John 15:10)

But whoso looketh into the perfect law of liberty, and continueth therein, he being not a forgetful hearer, but a doer of the work, this man shall be blessed in his deed. (Jas. 1:25)

And whatsoever we ask, we receive of him, because we keep his commandments, and do those things that are pleasing in his sight. (1 John 3:22)

For not the hearers of the law are just before God, but the doers of the law shall be justified. (Rom. 2:13)

Suggested Resources

Research obedience to God. We recommend the following:

Walking Wisely ☛ ◆
"Essential #4: Actively Obey and Apply God's Word" (86–90).
You will be advised to read other chapters with upcoming lessons in this book.

Our Father Abraham: Jewish Roots of the Christian Faith ♥
"The Problem with Judaizing" (24–26); "Salvation: By Grace or Works" (20–21); and "Paul and the Law" (27–28).

Recommended in: ◆ several lessons in this unit; ♥ several HOW unit studies. ☛ Key Resource for this unit.

Additional Reading

The Letter Writer: Paul's Background and Torah Perspective by Tim Hegg ♥
It is time for us to take a new and honest look at Paul as an apostle who was Torah observant, faithful to the call of Israel, and a great man that encouraged the followers of the Messiah to embrace the teachings of Moses and with great passion declared Yeshua to be the Messiah of Israel! The Letter Writer challenges traditional Christian viewpoints of the Apostle Paul, his message and the foundation of his theological approach and understanding. Through this remarkable book Tim Hegg attempts to re-establish a biblical, historical, and cultural understanding of Paul—the Torah observant Apostle. First Fruits of Zion. 332 pages ISBN 1892124165.

The Liberty of Obedience by Elisabeth Elliot
We often think that freedom means doing whatever we want, when we want. But true freedom comes from only one thing: obeying the Lord. Elisabeth Elliot calls on us to examine more closely our own obedience to God, measuring it in terms of our experience of his freedom, grace, and love. Elliot explains that we find the liberty of obedience through desire, dependence, and decision. Motivating and inspiring. Paperback - 94 pages (April 1987). Servant Publications; ISBN: 0892833580.

Nehemiah-Man of Radical Obedience by Marie Coody, Linda Shaw
In this ten-week Bible study of an often-overlooked Old Testament book, the authors link Nehemiah's obedience with its practical implications for believers today. As Nehemiah faced great opposition and numerous setbacks, he and the Israelites learned how to totally abandon themselves to God's will and way for their lives. Each lesson offers valuable observations to help deepen faith, inspire hope, and strengthen the resolve to follow God's leading at all costs. Paperback - 88 pages (1999). Beacon Hill Press; ISBN: 0834118203.

The Spirit of the Law by Ron Mosley
A straightforward and insightful approach to a difficult and sometimes perplexing subject. The book presents a fresh and liberating understanding of Jesus' and Paul's remarks about the Law, and in a way that the general public can easily relate to. Available online at http://www.haydid.org/spiritta.htm

Internet Sources

Family Bible Study: Obedience, Not Trumpets, Brought Down the Walls
Bible study on Joshua 6:1–27 from Baptist Standard.
http://www.baptiststandard.com/2001/9_10/pages/family.html

The Joy of Obedience
Excellent article by Charles Stanley of In Touch Ministries.
http://www.intouch.org/gen_content/index_627258_36081472.html

(i) *Law Written on the Heart*
Article from Bridges for Peace by Jim Gerrish, explaining that divine intention is that the Law would be perfectly fulfilled in each individual's life.
http://www.bridgesforpeace.com/publications/dispatch/ourjewishroots/Article-27.html

(i) *Torah Basics*
Article from First Fruit of Zion.
http://www.ffoz.org/TorahClub/torahbasics.shtml

Step 3: Expand

Choose and complete one or more of the following activities:

Activity 1: Write an Essay
In the lesson, "Acquiring Wisdom," you should have completed Activity 1, writing summary paragraphs for each of the four basic steps to acquiring wisdom. Use what you have learned in this lesson to expand the summary paragraph you wrote about "Obeying God's Word" into an essay on this topic. Refer to http://HeartofWisdom.com/Writing.htm.

Activity 2: Make a Chart
Make an obedience chart for yourself. Here's something to help you grow: If you have trouble obeying in simple things, for example, cleaning your room, obedience in the bigger things will be more difficult. Grade yourself on how well you obey in the simple, routine things of life. This will be just between you and God, so be honest with yourself. Make a chart with areas of obedience that you are expected to perform each week. This could include chores, choice of music or TV programs when your parents are not around, and so on. Grade yourself daily for a week by placing a star on each task that you obeyed well. Leave other areas blank if you didn't obey or didn't obey completely. At the end of the week, review your chart. How did you do? How was your attitude as you worked through these expectations? Based on these things, can God trust you to obey in the bigger things? If you find yourself lacking, don't condemn yourself. (Rom. 8:1 says ***There is therefore now no condemnation to those who are in Christ Jesus, who do not walk according to the flesh, but according to the Spirit.***) Rather, ask the Holy Spirit to help you grow in this area. Purpose to become an obedient person.

Activity 3: Write a Summary
What does the Bible say about disobedience? Read Heb. 13:17; Rom. 1:30; Eph. 6:6–7; 1 Sam. 15:23; Col. 3:20; Col. 3:22; Tit. 3:1. Next, read these verses and write a summary paragraph about the results of disobedience: Prov. 2:22; 10:7; 27–30; 17:2; 21:7; 28:9; Rom.1:28; Lev. 26:14–39; Prov. 1:28; Isa. 1:20.

Activity 4: Make a Chart
Make a chart showing how we are to obey God. List five columns titled: (1) From the Heart, (2) With Willingness, (3) Unreserved, (4) Enduring, and (5) Constant. Look up the

---

Recommended in: ◆ several lessons in this unit; ● several HOW unit studies. ☛ Key Resource for this unit.

following verses and write a summary to go under each column (verses are in order of titles): (1) Deut. 11:13; Rom. 6:17; (2) Ps. 18:44; Isa. 1:19; (3) Josh. 22:2, 3; (4) Deut. 28:14; (5) Phil. 2:12.

Activity 5: Make an Outline
Create an outline for *The Spirit of the Law* or write a summary for each chapter. *The Spirit of the Law* is available online. http://www.haydid.org/spiritta.htm

Activity 6: Make a Chart
Create a chart using the Bible characters listed below. Include the following columns: Person, Event, and Results. Write a summary of how each person was obedient and record the results in the chart. Alternative: Choose one person from the list below and write a paper on their obedience and the results. Include what would have happened if the person had not obeyed.

1. Noah (Gen. 6:22)
2. Abram (Gen. 12:1–4; Heb. 11:8; Gen. 22:3,12)
3. Caleb (Num. 32:12)
4. Asa (1 Kings 15:11)
5. Elijah (1 Kings 17:5)
6. Hezekiah (2 Kings 18:6)
7. Josiah (2 Kings 22:2)
8. David (Ps. 119:106)
9. Zerubbabel (Hag. 1:12)
10. Joseph (Matt. 1:24)
11. Zacharias &c. (Luke 1:6)
12. Paul (Acts 26:19)

Activity 7: Help Another
Practice obedience by showing love in action. Read Matt. 22:39; John 17:22; 1 Cor. 16:14; 1 Pet. 1:22; 1 John 3:23. Pray about helping others. Ask God to reveal a needy person to you. Can you help with chores or home repairs, take a meal to someone, or offer child care? What is the cost of discipleship? Read and paraphrase Jesus' words in Luke 19:11–28.

Activity 8: Write a Paper
Write and present a one-page paper about Timothy and his godly training. See 2 Tim. 1:5 and 3:15–16.

Activity 9: Discuss
A.W. Tozer said, "To escape the error of salvation by works we have fallen into the opposite error of salvation without obedience." What do you think he meant? Can you give an example?

Activity 10: Learn Hebrew and Greek Words
The Hebrew verb translated "obey" is *sama' bᵉ*, lit. "hearken to." The verb used in the NT is *hypakouo* (noun, *hypakoe*; adjective, *hypekoos*), a compound of *akouo*, which also means "hear." *Hypakouo* means literally "hear under." The NT also uses *esakouo* (1 Cor. 14:21), lit. "hear *into*," *peithomai*, and *peitharcheo* (Tit. 3:1) (Wood 1996).

Activity 11: Copy Verses
Copy at least ten of the verses listed in Step 2. Title the paper "Obedience." Add it to your portfolio.

Step 4: Excel

Memorize Matt. 5:17. Discuss your understanding of how Jesus fulfilled the Law and the Prophets.

The King James Version	Amplified Bible	The New Century Version	The New Living Translation
Think not that I am come to destroy the law, or the prophets: I am not come to destroy, but to fulfil.	Do not think that I have come to do away with or undo the Law or the Prophets; I have come not to do away with or undo but to complete and fulfill them.	Don't think that I have come to destroy the law of Moses or the teaching of the prophets. I have not come to destroy them but to bring about what they said.	Don't misunderstand why I have come. I did not come to abolish the law of Moses or the writings of the prophets. No, I came to fulfill them.

The word translated "destroy" (KJV) in this verse is the Greek word *kataluo*, which means "destroy, demolish, dismantle," more specifically "do away with, abolish, annul, make invalid." The "prophets" refer to commentators upon the Law.

The Greek word "fulfill" means to complete, be completely, , full degree, cause something to be full, make complete, make total, finish complete an activity, provide fully, supply all needed, proclaim completely, tell fully, give true meaning, cause to happen. (Dictionary of Biblical Languages with Semantic Domains: Greek)

Are there aspects of this concept that are difficult for you to understand? Think of it this way: If a man jumps off a bridge, he does not destroy or break the law of gravity. He fulfills it, or proves it.

Read the verse in context (read the rest of the chapter). Ask your parents to help you discover Bible verses that bring this truth alive inside you. When you have found portions of Scripture that minister to you about this topic, write them down in your portfolio. Read them daily and meditate on the truth contained in them. Talk with a parent often to discuss your ideas and questions about obedience.

Recommended in: ◆ several lessons in this unit; ● several HOW unit studies. ☛ Key Resource for this unit.

Praying for Wisdom LS10107

Step 1: Excite

There are numerous Scriptures which tell us that God gives us wisdom through the Holy Spirit. Memorize Jas. 1:5–8, which says: *If any of you lacks wisdom, he should ask God, who gives generously to all without finding fault, and it will be given to him. But when he asks, he must believe and not doubt, because he who doubts is like a wave of the sea, blown and tossed by the wind. That man should not think he will receive anything from the Lord; he is a double-minded man, unstable in all he does.*

Do you lack wisdom in certain areas of your life? Take a minute to ask God for wisdom in those areas. Believe that you receive when you ask.

Step 2: Examine

To pray for wisdom is to come to God in humility, acknowledging our need for His wisdom. The world often looks down on the one who acknowledges his weaknesses. God will never find fault in a prayer from a humble heart, for *God opposes the proud, but gives grace to the humble* (Jas. 4:6).

God promises: *For everyone who asks receives, and he who seeks finds, and to him who knocks it will be opened* (Matt. 7:8). A person will be blessed when their mind is focused on a prevailing spiritual and eternal interest, one that keeps steady in its purposes for God. That person will grow wise by afflictions, will continue fervent in devotion, and will rise above trials and oppositions.

In Eph. 1:17–20, Paul prays for the church of Ephesus to receive wisdom. Memorize the following verses:

That the God of our Lord Jesus Christ, the Father of glory, may give unto you the spirit of wisdom and revelation in the knowledge of him: The eyes of your understanding being enlightened; that ye may know what is the hope of his calling, and what the riches of the glory of his inheritance in the saints, And what is the exceeding greatness of his power to us-ward who believe, according to the working of his mighty power, Which he wrought in Christ, when he raised him from the dead, and set him at his own right hand in the heavenly places.

Jeremiah 23 explains the results of choosing to apart from the counsel of God. Verse 22 says, *But if they had stood in My counsel, then they would have announced My words to My people, and would have turned them back from their evil way and from the evil of their deeds.* Read Job 28:12–28; Prov. 3:13–18; Rom. 1:22; 16:27; and 1 Cor. 1:17–21; 2:6–8.

When I first became a Christian my Grandmother gave me the book *The Kneeling Christian*. I was absolutely amazed at the promises of prayer in the Bible. Here is an excerpt from this powerful little book:

> "WHEN we stand with Christ in glory, looking o'er life's finished story," the most amazing feature of that life as it is looked back upon will be its prayerlessness. We shall be almost beside ourselves with astonishment that we spent so little time in real intercession. It will be our turn to "wonder."

In our Lord's last discourse to His loved ones, just before the most wonderful of all prayers, the Master again and again held out His kingly golden sceptre and said, as it were, "What is your request? It shall be granted unto you, even unto the whole of My kingdom!"

Do we believe this? We must do so if we believe our Bibles. Shall we just read over very quietly and thoughtfully one of our Lord's promises, reiterated so many times? If we had never read them before, we should open our eyes in bewilderment, for these promises are almost incredible. From the lips of any mere man they would be quite unbelievable. But it is the Lord of heaven and earth Who speaks; and He is speaking at the most solemn moment of His life. It is the eve of His death and passion. It is a farewell message. Now listen!

Verily, verily I say unto you, he that believeth on Me, the works that I do shall he do also; and greater works than these shall he do: because I go unto the Father. And whatsoever ye shall ask in My name, that will I do, that the Father may be glorified in the Son. If ye shall ask anything in My name, that will I do. (John 14:13, 14). Now, could any words be plainer or clearer than these? Could any promise be greater or grander? Has anyone else, anywhere, at any time, ever offered so much?

How staggered those disciples must have been! Surely they could scarcely believe their own ears. But that promise is made also to you and to me. And, lest there should be any mistake on their part, or on ours, our Lord repeats Himself a few moments afterwards.

Yes, and the Holy Spirit bids John record those words again. *If ye abide in Me, and My words abide in you, ask whatsoever ye will, and it shall be done unto you. Herein is My Father glorified, that ye bare much fruit; and so shall ye be My disciples"* (John 25:7, 8).

These words are of such grave importance, and so momentous, that the Savior of the world is not content even with a threefold utterance of them. He urges His disciples to obey His command "*to ask.*" In fact, He tells them that one sign of their being His "friends" will be the obedience to His commands in all things (verse 14). Then He once more repeats His wishes: "*Ye did not choose Me, but I chose you, and appointed you, that ye should go and bear fruit, and that your fruit should abide: that whatsoever ye shall ask the Father, in My name, He may give it you"* (John 25:16).

One would think that our Lord had now made it plain enough that He wanted them to pray; that He needed their prayers, and that without prayer they could accomplish nothing. But to our intense surprise He returns again to the same subject, saying very much the same words.

Verily, verily I say unto you, if ye ask anything of the Father, He will give it you in My name. Hitherto have ye asked nothing in My name: ask, and ye shall receive, that your joy may be fulfilled" (John 26:23, 24).

Never before had our Lord laid such stress on any promise or command—never! This truly marvelous promise is given us six times over. Six times, almost in the same breath, our Savior commands us to ask whatsoever we will. This is the greatest—the most wonderful—promise ever made to man. Yet most men—Christian men—practically ignore it! Is it not so?

Recommended in: ◆ several lessons in this unit; ◗ several HOW unit studies. ◗━ Key Resource for this unit.

The exceeding greatness of the promise seems to overwhelm us. Yet we know that He is *"able to do exceeding abundantly above all that we ask or think"* (Eph. 3:20).

So our blessed Master gives the final exhortation, before He is seized, and bound, and scourged, before His gracious lips are silenced on the cross, *Ye shall ask in My name . . . for the Father Himself loveth you* (verse 26). We have often spent much time in reflecting upon our Lord's seven words from the cross. And it is well we should do so. Have we ever spent one hour in meditating upon this, our Savior's sevenfold invitation to pray?

Today He sits on the throne of His Majesty on high, and He holds out to us the sceptre of His power. Shall we touch it and tell Him our desires? He bids us take of His treasures. He yearns to grant us *"according to the riches of His glory,"* that we may *"be strengthened with power through His Spirit in the inner man."* He tells us that our strength and our fruitfulness depend upon prayers. He reminds us that our very joy depends upon answered prayer (John 26: 24).

And yet we allow the devil to persuade us to neglect prayer! He makes us believe that we can do more by our own efforts than by our prayers—by our intercourse with men than by our intercession with God. It passes one's comprehension that so little heed should be given to our Lord's sevenfold invitation—command—promise! How dare we work for Christ without being much on our knees?

Fellow laborers in His vineyard, it is quite evident that our Master desires us to ask, and to ask much. He tells us we glorify God by doing so! Nothing is beyond the scope of prayer which is not beyond the will of God—and we do not desire to go beyond His will.

We dare not say that our Lord's words are not true. Yet somehow or other few Christians really seem to believe them. What holds us back? What seals our lips? What keeps us from making much of prayer? Do we doubt His love? Never! He gave His life for us and to us. Do we doubt the Father's love? Nay. "The Father Himself loveth you," said Christ when urging His disciples to pray.

Do we doubt His power? Not for a moment. Hath He not said, *"All power hath been given unto Me in heaven and on earth. Go ye . . . and lo, I am with you alway . . ."*? (Matt. 28:18-20). Do we doubt His wisdom? Do we mistrust His choice for us? Not for a moment. And yet so very few of His followers consider prayer really worth while. Of course, they would deny this—but actions speak louder than words. Are we afraid to put God to the test? He has said we may do so. "Bring Me the whole tithe into the storehouse . . . and prove Me now herewith, saith the Lord of Hosts, if I will not open you the windows of heaven, and pour you out a blessing that there shall not be room enough to receive it" (Mal. 3:10). Whenever God makes us a promise, let us boldly say, as did Paul, I believe God (Acts 27:25), and trust Him to keep His word.

Shall we begin today to be men of prayer, if we have never done so before? Let us not put it off till a more convenient season. God wants me to pray. The dear Savior wants me to pray. He needs my prayers. So much—in fact, everything—depends upon prayer.

Suggested Resources

Below are more resources on praying for wisdom.

Walking Wisely ⌐— ◆
Chapter 4, "The Essentials for Walking in Wisdom" (67–110). If you read this chapter in the last lesson, reread pages 75–76.

Additional Reading

The Kneeling Christian (written anonymously) ●
This is one of my favorite books (see excerpt in this lesson). Prayer, although an essential ingredient of the Christian experience, remains mysterious and foreign to many Christians. Realizing this, the author set about to familiarize believers with the source of power available to them through prayer. According to *The Kneeling Christian*, all real growth in the spiritual life—all victory over temptation, all confidence and peace in the presence of difficulties and dangers, all repose of spirit in times of great disappointment of loss, all habitual communion with God—depends upon the practice of secret prayer. Paperback - 128 pages (1986). Zondervan Publishing House; ISBN: 0310334918.

Proverbs Prayers: Praying the Wisdom of Proverbs into Your Life Every Day by John Mason
People say that Proverbs is their favorite book in the Bible because it helps them daily in many practical ways. When readers open this book, they will find themselves reading a Proverb and then praying a heartfelt prayer that includes principles and promises from the chapter. Every thirty-one days, readers can pray all of the wisdom of Proverbs over their lives. This book will become any reader's best friend, helping them find strength, peace, and answers to a better life! Hardcover - 133 pages (2000). Insight International; ISBN: 1890900117.

Step 3: Expand

Choose and complete one or more of the following activities:

Activity 1: Write a Prayer
Compose a prayer, asking God for wisdom. Remembering that God loves you and prayer is communication between you and Him, make your prayer as intimate and personal as you wish. This activity may be kept private if you so desire.

Activity 2: Write an Essay
In the "Acquiring Wisdom" lesson you should have completed Activity 1, writing summary paragraphs for each of the four basic steps to acquiring wisdom. Use what you have learned in this lesson to expand the summary paragraph you wrote about "Pray for Wisdom" into an essay on this topic. Refer to http://HeartofWisdom.com/Writing.htm.

Recommended in: ◆ several lessons in this unit; ● several HOW unit studies. ⌐— Key Resource for this unit.

Activity 3: Make a Collage
Using family pictures and magazines, make a collage of people that you consider to be wise. These people may include family members or famous people. In the center of your collage, write down a simple prayer that these people may have prayed regarding wisdom.

Activity 4: Create a Book
Using an exhaustive concordance, do a word search on *wisdom* in the Bible. How many examples can you find of someone who actually prayed for wisdom? Make a book of remembrance that includes each of the instances you can find. Include the person's name as a page heading, an excerpt from Scripture in which he/she asked for wisdom, and a brief summary of the biblical example. Each person should take only one page.

Activity 5: Write a Commentary
Write your own commentary on the verses below. Write as if you were explaining these passages to a child.

Ask, and it shall be given you; seek, and ye shall find; knock, and it shall be opened unto you (Matt. 7:7).

And I say unto you, Ask, and it shall be given you; seek, and ye shall find; knock, and it shall be opened unto you. For every one that asketh receiveth; and he that seeketh findeth; and to him that knocketh it shall be opened (Luke 11:9–10).

Step 4: Excel

In Jas. 1:5, "Let him ask" is translated from the Greek word, *aiteitw*. It is a present active imperative of *aitew* that means "let him keep on asking." Our minds are nothing compared to the mind of God. His wisdom and ability far exceeds that of man. When we come to the end of ourselves and don't know what to do, we can ask God for wisdom. Operate with the mind of God and with His wisdom. He has provided wisdom to help you, but you must ask. Purpose to pray for wisdom regularly. Make it a habit to pray for wisdom before your Bible study each day.

"The Ephesian Prayers" are some of the most powerful prayers in the Bible. You should get into the habit of praying them every day. Copy Ephesians 1:17–20 onto a card (see below) and use it to pray for your parents, future spouse, or others needing wisdom. Pray these Scriptures for yourself as well:

Dear God,

Give unto _____ the spirit of wisdom and revelation in the knowledge of you. Let the eyes of _____'s understanding be enlightened; that _____ may know what is the hope of his calling, and what the riches of the glory of his inheritance in the saints, And what is the exceeding greatness of his power to us-ward who believe, according to the working of his mighty power, Which he wrought in Christ, when he raised him from the dead, and set him at his own right hand in the heavenly places.

Set a goal to seek God's wisdom for your life. Once you learn the principles of godly wisdom, God will apply these to your life in a miraculous way. As He makes Himself known to you, your relationship with Him will grow and deepen.

Managing Conflict Wisely LS10108

Step 1: Excite

How well do you handle criticism? Have you ever had anyone unjustly criticize you for something? Talk about it. What happened? How did you feel? Did you feel sad, hurt, angry, betrayed? Did you lash out or say something you later regretted? Did you apologize? Did you feel like crying in frustration? Did you become more loving because you faced conflict? Did you become resentful?

Step 2: Examine

All of us face conflict at some point. We must be ready for it when it comes. In your life, the biggest difficulties you will face are not conflicts in relationships, or disappointment. The real root of the problem is our sinful nature which is self-centered and prideful, and causes us to be defensive when we don't get what we want or expect. Satan will try to discourage you from pursuing God by making you feel defeated and confused. But no matter how injured you feel or what your past holds, the truth is that God loves you and has a good plan for your life (Jer. 29:11).

God's Word gives us direction in how to handle conflicts. God wants us to handle conflicts by being tolerant instead of difficult, by showing kindness and helping others. He does not want us to feel sorry for ourselves. Christian character is formed in us by the experiential process of our being conformed to the image of Christ.

The Sermon on the Mount, also called the Beatitudes, consists of a detailed description of God's ethical standards. The word *beatitude* is derived from the Latin *beatus*, which means "blessed" or "happy." These principles reflect God's nature and reveal His will. The first part of the Beatitudes (verses 3–6) focuses on our relationship with God. The rest of the verses (7–10) are about our relationships with others. This pattern reflects Jesus' core message: *"The first commandment is to love God with all your heart and soul and mind, and the second commandment is to love your neighbor as yourself."*

> *Blessed are the poor in spirit: for theirs is the kingdom of heaven. Blessed are they that mourn: for they shall be comforted. Blessed are the meek: for they shall inherit the earth. Blessed are they which do hunger and thirst after righteousness: for they shall be filled. Blessed are the merciful: for they shall obtain mercy. Blessed are the pure in heart: for they shall see God. Blessed are the peacemakers: for they shall be called the children of God. Blessed are they which are persecuted for righteousness' sake: for theirs is the kingdom of heaven. Blessed are ye, when men shall revile you, and persecute you, and shall say all manner of evil against you falsely, for my sake. Rejoice, and be exceeding glad: for great is your reward in heaven: for so persecuted they the prophets which were before you. (Matt. 5:3–12)*

The Beatitudes relate to how we should handle conflict. If someone told condemning lies about you unjustly, your natural inclination would be to feel angry, hurt, and resentful. But Jesus tells us that we are blessed when we are criticized. He said, *"Blessed are ye, when men shall revile you, and persecute you, and shall say all manner of evil against you falsely, for my sake"* (Matt. 5:11). Examine this verse in different Bible versions.

Recommended in: ◆ several lessons in this unit; ● several HOW unit studies. ◉— Key Resource for this unit.

The New International Version	American Standard Version	Amplified Bible
"Blessed are you when people insult you, persecute you and falsely say all kinds of evil against you because of me.	Blessed are ye when men shall reproach you, and persecute you, and say all manner of evil against you falsely, for my sake.	Blessed (happy, to be envied, and spiritually prosperous—with life joy and satisfaction in God's favor and salvation, regardless of your outward conditions) are you when people revile you and persecute you and say all kinds of evil things against you falsely on My account.

The Bible shows us that conflict can provide a unique opportunity to better understand other persons' opinions and values. God can use conflict to help us better understand ourselves and one another. When we face conflict we need to ask, "What might God want to teach me through these difficult people?"

James says that trials should not be seen as a punishment, a curse, or a calamity, but as something that must prompt rejoicing. Furthermore, they should produce *pure* joy (lit., "all joy"; i.e., joy that is full or unmixed), not just *some* joy coupled with much grief.

James, a servant of God and of the Lord Jesus Christ, to the twelve tribes which are scattered abroad, greeting. My brethren, count it all joy when ye fall into divers temptations; Knowing this, that the trying of your faith worketh patience. But let patience have her perfect work, that ye may be perfect and entire, wanting nothing (Jas. 1:1–4).

Examine this passage in different Bible versions.

The New International Version	American Standard Version	Amplified Bible
Consider it pure joy, my brothers, whenever you face trials of many kinds, because you know that the testing of your faith develops perseverance. Perseverance must finish its work so that you may be mature and complete, not lacking anything.	Count it all joy, my brethren, when ye fall into manifold temptations; Knowing that the proving of your faith worketh patience. And let patience have its perfect work, that ye may be perfect and entire, lacking in nothing.	Consider it wholly joyful, my brethren, whenever you are enveloped in or encounter trials of any sort or fall into various temptations. Be assured *and* understand that the trial *and* proving of your faith bring out endurance *and* steadfastness *and* patience. But let endurance *and* steadfastness *and* patience have full play *and* do a thorough work, so that you may be [people] perfectly and fully developed [with no defects], lacking in nothing.

Many times, people who have a deep spiritual life have suffered in some ways which seem greatly unfair. If you asked them what they learned during their troubled periods, they would tell you that they grew spiritually. Their faith produced, through the grace of God, perseverance.

Christ experienced wounds, pain, unfairness, injustice, and hatred. He learned obedience from what he suffered and became *the author of eternal salvation unto all them that obey him.*

Who in the days of his flesh, when he had offered up prayers and supplications with strong crying and tears unto him that was able to save him from death, and was heard in that he feared; Though he were a Son, yet learned he obedience by the things which he suffered; And being made perfect, he became the author of eternal salvation unto all them that obey him (Heb. 5:7–9).

Salvation does *not* promise an easy life. We can still expect difficulties and trials. God's Word tells us that we should have joy, even though *now for a little while you may have had to suffer grief in all kinds of trials* (1 Pet. 1:6). Conflict and criticism are not meant to cause us to stumble, but to reveal the substance of our faith. Jesus Himself was not immune to suffering. And we are called to walk in His steps.

> *Beloved, think it not strange concerning the fiery trial which is to try you, as though some strange thing happened unto you: But rejoice, inasmuch as ye are partakers of Christ's sufferings; that, when his glory shall be revealed, ye may be glad also with exceeding joy. If ye be reproached for the name of Christ, happy are ye; for the spirit of glory and of God resteth upon you: on their part he is evil spoken of, but on your part he is glorified.* (1 Pet. 4:12–14)

Suggested Resources

Below are more resources on managing conflicts:

Walking Wisely ●— ◆
Chapter 8, "Wisdom in Times of Conflict and Criticism" (203–219). You will be advised to read other chapters with upcoming lessons in this book.

Additional Reading

A Path Through Suffering by Elisabeth Elliot
No stranger to pain, grief, and loss, Elisabeth Elliot helps navigate the treacherous path for those who feel helplessly lost. Through suffering, she says there is only one reliable path. It is steep and narrow. But that path transforms all tragedies into something wonderful beyond imagining, for suffering is one way a merciful God draws us to himself and expands our capacity for intimacy, surrender, and obedience. Paperback - 200 pages (1992). Servant Publications; ISBN: 0892838019.

As We Forgive Those by Elisabeth Elliot
When hurts and wrongs separate us from others, is there any way back to a restored relationship? Can the forgiveness we find in Christ affect our life with others? Forgiveness is more than a vague feeling of good will, says Elisabeth Elliot. It is self-denial and an unconquerable force of love. In fact, forgiving others is essential to spiritual growth and victory. Paperback (1992) Back To The Bible; ISBN: 0847411893.

Recommended in: ◆ several lessons in this unit; ● several HOW unit studies. ●— Key Resource for this unit.

Video

Suffering Is Not for Nothing Volumes 1 & 2, Video by Elisabeth Elliot
Through the centuries, Christian philosophers have pondered the mysteries of the knowledge of God and the knowledge of self. With keen insight, the widow of martyred missionary Jim Elliot penetrates the world's mediocrity and popular panaceas for anxiety and confusion. She raises a standard for excellence straight from the pages of Scripture. True peace, contentment, and freedom from worldly despair, she maintains, is found in the clarity of biblical wisdom and intimacy with Christ.

Internet Sources

Conflict: Friend or Foe
Article explaining that conflict provides a unique opportunity to better understand other persons' opinions and values.
http://www.backtothebible.org/lifeissues/relationships/conflict_friend_foe.html

How Do You Define Conflict?
Article explaining that conflict is the opposing positions of two individuals on the same subject.
http://wordtruth.com/conflict35.htm

How to Handle Conflict & Criticism Wisely
Charles Stanley explains that believers led by the Spirit of God cannot avoid confrontation. God has a specific way for you to handle every conflict that arises.
http://www.intouch.org/myintouch/exploring/bible_says/difficulties/conflict_144325.html

Hurt by Someone
An excellent article by Elisabeth Elliot. Mrs. Elliot's husband was killed by people from a tribe he was serving on the mission field. Mrs. Elliot witnessed to her husband's murderer and he came to salvation as did most of the tribe.
http://www.backtothebible.org/lifeissues/relationships/hurt_by_someone.html

Step 3: Expand

Choose and complete one or more of the following activities:

Activity 1: Copy and Memorize Bible Passages
Copy all the Bible verses in this lesson into your portfolio. The verses in this lesson are excellent to have stored in your memory for times of trouble. Choose at least one passage to memorize.

Activity 2: Conduct an Interview
Interview three people you admire. Ask them to tell you about a time of conflict in their life and how God revealed Himself to them during it. It will bless you to hear their answers and bless them to share their memories.

Activity 3: Write Summaries
Use Bible study tools to do research. Write a description for each of the following Beatitudes (Matthew chapter 5):

The poor in spirit (verse 3)
They who mourn (verse 4)
The meek (verse 5)
They that hunger and thirst after justice (verse 6)
The merciful (verse 7)
The clean of heart (verse 8)
The peacemakers (verse 9)
They that suffer persecution for justice' sake (verse 10)

Activity 4: Write a Personal Essay
Write about a time of conflict in your life. Explain how you felt and how you handled the problem. Describe the resolution of the conflict and what you learned from the experience. Refer to http://HeartofWisdom.com/Writing.htm.

Activity 5: Create Art
Choose one of the Bible passages from this lesson. Copy the passage in your best handwriting, in calligraphy, or onto the computer in fancy type. Mount the verse on a plaque or place it in a frame (with a matte) to display in your home or bedroom as a reminder of God's love in times of conflict.

Step 4: Excel

What did you learn about conflict? Did you learn anything about God's perspective of conflict? Share the most important or profound thing you learned in this lesson.

Set specific goals regarding accepting and learning from conflict in your own life. When faced with a conflict, pause briefly and ask God to help you use it as an opportunity for learning, growing, and increasing maturity.

Recommended in: ◆ several lessons in this unit; ◆ several HOW unit studies.   ◉— Key Resource for this unit.

Seeking Wise Counsel LS10109

Step 1: Excite

Wisdom means understanding the consequences of our actions and words before we act or speak. Wisdom means having the knowledge and understanding to recognize the right course of action, and having the will and courage to follow it. When we allow wisdom to have this good work in our lives, we become people of character. It takes a person of real character to act in the way that wisdom dictates he should act.

How many wise people do you know? Make a list. What are their character traits? Ask your parents if they would consider anyone on your list wise enough to go to for counsel. While you are young you have your parents for counsel. When you get older you might not have that option. Do you think you would appear on someone's "wise list"? Which do you think is more important: wealth or a good name?

Step 2: Examine

On occasion everyone will need to ask for advise, even Kings. In the book of Daniel, chapter 2, King Nebuchadnezzar has a dream and sought advice from his counsel. He gathered his advisors and commanded them to interpret his dream without revealing the dream to them. They said, *"Let the king tell his servants the dream. The counselors answered before the king, and said, "There is not a man upon the earth that can shew the king's matter: therefore there is no king, lord, nor ruler, that asked such things at any magician, or astrologer, or Chaldean. And it is a rare thing that the king requireth, and there is none other that can shew it before the king, except the gods, whose dwelling is not with flesh. ?" For this cause the king was angry and very furious, and commanded to destroy all the wise men of Babylon.*

No regular man had wise counsel for the King. However God revealed the meaning of the dream to His faithful servant Daniel. The secret dream *was revealed unto Daniel in a night vision. Then Daniel blessed the God of heaven. Daniel answered and said, Blessed be the name of God for ever and ever: for wisdom and might are his:? And he changeth the times and the seasons: he removeth kings, and setteth up kings: he giveth wisdom unto the wise, and knowledge to them that know understanding:? He revealeth the deep and secret things: he knoweth what is in the darkness, and the light dwelleth with him.? I thank thee, and praise thee, O thou God of my fathers, who hast given me wisdom and might, and hast made known unto me now what we desired of thee: for thou hast now made known unto us the king's matter.?*

Daniel told the King the interpretation of the dream. Within seven years, Daniel's words came to pass. Daniel's qualifications recognized Daniel as a prophet of God. There is a strong test for a prophet. What the prophet predicts must always come true! If his prophecy does not come to pass, then his words should be ignored.

...How shall we know the word which the LORD hath not spoken? When a prophet speaketh in the name of the LORD, if the thing follow not, nor come to pass, that is the thing which the LORD hath not spoken, but the prophet hath spoken it presumptuously: thou shalt not be afraid of him. (Dt 18:20-22).

We can follow wisdom's path by first learning God's will through reading and studying His Word. We can also listen to wise counsel. When we seek counsel from someone they must be in tune with God, faithful, and obedient to His Word. We find wise counsel by finding a person of godly character. Biblical wisdom has no correlation to a person's IQ or education, because it is a matter of spiritual understanding. It has to do with character and values; it means looking at the world through the grid of God's truth. A counselor is a wise man, versed in law and diplomacy (1 Chr. 27:32,33). A mature Christian friend can help pray and give you insight in a decision-making process.

Proverbs is full of direction about receiving and giving counsel. Our actions affect others. What we speak can have one of two effects: it can either uplift and encourage or cast down and discourage.

The words of a wise man's mouth are gracious . . . (Eccl. 10:12). Warren Wiersbe talks about the many references to the tongue in Proverbs (*Wiersbe's Expository Outlines on the Old Testament*)

> There are blessings of a godly tongue. (This demands a godly heart, because the tongue only speaks what the heart treasures.) When used for good, [counsel and friendship] the tongue is like valuable silver (10:20); a beautiful and fruitful tree of life (15:4; see 12:14 and 18:20); a refreshing well of water (18:4; 10:11); and a healthy dose of medicine (12:18). See also James 3. The tongue should be used for right purposes: Bringing peace (15:1,26); giving wise reproof to the erring (25:12; 28:23); delivering lost souls from death (11:9; 14:3-5,25; 12:6); teaching people the things of the Lord (15:7; 16:21,23; 20:15); and carrying the good news of the Gospel (25:25). . . . It is sobering to realize that the tongue can be used to damage reputations and cause trouble, when it ought to be used to praise God, pray, and witness to others about Christ. The tongue is a "little member" of the body (Jam, 3:5), but it is one member that must be yielded to God as a tool of righteousness (Rom. 6:12-13).

Read and discuss the following verses:

Hear counsel, and receive instruction, that thou mayest be wise in thy latter end. (Prov. 19:20)

He who walks with wise men will be wise, but the companion of fools will suffer harm. (Prov. 13:20)

A wise man will hear, and will increase learning; and a man of understanding shall attain unto wise counsels. (Prov. 1:5)

Give instruction to a wise man, and he will be yet wiser: teach a just man, and he will increase in learning. (Prov. 9:9)

Where no counsel is, the people fall: but in the multitude of counsellors there is safety. (Prov. 11:14)

Recommended in: ♦ several lessons in this unit; ♥ several HOW unit studies.　☛ Key Resource for this unit.

The way of a fool is right in his own eyes: but he that hearkeneth unto counsel is wise. (Prov. 12:15)

Without counsel purposes are disappointed: but in the multitude of counsellors they are established. (Prov. 15:22)

Every purpose is established by counsel: and with good advice make war. (Prov. 20:18)

For by wise counsel thou shalt make thy war: and in multitude of counsellors there is safety. (Prov. 24:6)

Ointment and perfume rejoice the heart: so doth the sweetness of a man's friend by hearty counsel. (Prov. 27:9)

People are not born with high standards that result in strong character. Rather, parents train and equip their children and children *become* persons of godly character over a process of time. Anyone can make choices that will eventually cause them to be either a person of high character or a person with no character.

Prov. 22:1 says *"A good name is to be chosen rather than great riches..."*

The King James Version	The New International Version	Amplified Bible	Today's English Version
A good name is rather to be chosen than great riches, and loving favour rather than silver and gold.	A good name is more desirable than great riches; to be esteemed is better than silver or gold.	A GOOD name is rather to be chosen than great riches, and loving favor rather than silver and gold.	If you have to choose between a good reputation and great wealth, choose a good reputation.

Although this verse is often used on name tags and other things that declare our actual name, the meaning of this passage of Scripture has often been interpreted with much more significance than the spelling of *John, Mary,* or *Susie.* A good name—i.e., a good reputation or character—is to be chosen. When you have established yourself as a person of character, your name will be known. When people hear your name in business deals, academic activities, and community service, they will immediately speak highly of you. Word of a good reputation gets around; unfortunately, so does word of a bad one.

Are you a person of good character? Here's a quick test for you. Answer yes or no to the following ten questions. Keep in mind that this is not an all-inclusive character analysis. This simply covers some issues that your character will dictate your responses.

1. Do you do what you say you will do—even to your own hurt?
2. Are you honest all the time, even if it costs you money, time, or a good grade?
3. Do you respect and show honor to your parents and other elders?
4. Do you dress modestly?

5. Will you stand up publicly for what is right according to God's standards?
6. Do you honor God in how you live?
7. Do you refrain from gossip, no matter how tempting the story might be?
8. Are you committed to remaining sexually pure?
9. Do you keep job commitments (such as babysitting) even when something comes up that you would rather do? And do you give adequate notice if you really *must* cancel?
10. Do you openly respect and honor the things of God as well as men and women of God?

This quiz is not foolproof, but it will give you some indication of whether or not you are on the road to becoming an adult with good character. If you answered yes to all of the questions, you are well on your way. Any negative answers will represent areas for you to work on. Get a parent to help you become strong in these areas of your life. Determine that you will have a good name.

Suggested Resources

Below are resources about associating with and receiving counsel from wise people.

Gaining Favor with God and Man by William M. Thayer
Description (see additional information in Resources section): Each chapter contains complete short stories about great men, their wisdom, and their characters. Each page is dripping with wisdom from a Christian perspective.

Our Father Abraham: Jewish Roots of the Christian Faith ●
Read about wise men and the Hebrew view of wisdom (281–282).

Walking Wisely ●— ◆
"Essential #7: Associate and Learn from Wise People" (101–109). You will be advised to read other chapters with upcoming lessons in this book.

Internet Source

Discovering God's Will
This article by Charles Stanley helps answer the questions: How do I discern the counsel of others in knowing God's will? How do I know what role circumstances have in understanding God's will for me?
http://www.intouch.org/myintouch/exploring/bible_says/God_Will/counsel_146164.html

Nathan the Prophet
Nathan counseled and rebuked King David.
http://www.execulink.com/~wblank/20010729.htm

Without Counsel
Bibly study on Genesis 41:1-8 where Pharaoh seeks counsel from Joseph.
http://www.inhymn.com/devotions/Genesis/genesis_189.htm

Recommended in: ◆ several lessons in this unit; ● several HOW unit studies. ●— Key Resource for this unit.

(i) *Wise Counsel*
A Quiet Time Bible study about Jethro, Moses' father-in-law.
http://www.gospelcom.net/ivpress/bible/exodus/exodus11.shtml

(i) *Wise Counsel*
Bible Study from Genesis 41:37-57. Pharaoh seeks wisdom from Joseph.
http://www.usethesword.com/gens69.html

(i) *Godly Counsel*
Brief article from Mustard Seed.
http://www.mustardseed.net/html/togodlycounsel.html

Step 3: Expand

Choose and complete one or more of the following activities:

Activity 1: Take a Test
Copy the quiz listed in Step 2. Take the quiz, then draw up a list of areas you feel might need some attention in your life. Ask a parent to pray with you, asking the Lord for maturity in any areas of weakness.

Activity 2: Become a Bible Character
Find a person from the Bible whom you could go to for wise counsel. Study this person's life and write a speech that this person could have given on the subject of character. Dress as this person would have dressed in his time and present the speech to parents, family, or your homeschooling group.

Activity 3: Do a Word Study
Choose five positive characteristics of a godly person. Use a concordance to find two or three verses dealing with each trait. Write a summary on each one.

Activity 4: Read Scripture
One way to become wise is to associate with wise people, including companions and teachers. Conversely, to associate with fools brings problems. The Hebrew words for *companion* (ro'eh) and *suffers harm* (yeroa') sound a bit alike. The influence of good and bad associations is a common theme in Proverbs (1:10–11; 2:12; 4:14–17; 16:29; 22:24–25; 23:20–21; 28:7). (Walvoord, J. F. 1983). Look up and read the listed verses.

Activity 5: Paraphrase
Read Prov. 3:13-18, and then write it in your own words. Discuss your paraphrase with a friend. Refer to http://HeartofWisdom.com/Writing.htm.

Activity 6: Make a List
Read 1 Cor. 12 and 1 John 4. Make a list of character qualities of a godly person.

Activity 7: Copy Verses
Copy all ten of the verses listed in step 2. Title the paper "Wise Counsel." Add it to your Portfolio.

Step 4: Excel

Your parents are counselors given to you by God (Deut. 4:9; 11:19; Isa. 38:19; Prov. 22:6; Eph. 6:4). Colossians 3:20 tells children to *obey your parents in all things, for this is well-pleasing to the Lord.* Eph 6:1 says *Children, obey your parents in the Lord: for this is right.* The word "obey" in this verse means in the Greek:

1 To listen attentively
2 To heed or conform to a command or authority

Exodus 20:12 says *Honor thy father and thy mother: that thy days may be long upon the land which the Lord thy God giveth thee.* (Ex. 20:12). This is the first of God's commandments with a promise. God says if you honor your parents you will have a long life and it will be well with you.

How do you honor your parents? One way is to obey them. Remember, Obedience is the great factor in our whole relationship to God. *Obey my voice, and I will be your God* (Jer. 7.23; 11.4).

One who truly honors their authority does so out of an act of respect. When you need direction go to them for counsel. Who better to ask then the counselor God personally gave to you! God has placed our parent's in authority over our lives to teach us. If we love the Lord and want to seek him, we ought to seek out our parent's counsel.

Write a letter to your parents thanking them for their counsel. Include specific instances in which you benefited from their wise words.

Recommended in: ◆ several lessons in this unit; ● several HOW unit studies. ●━ Key Resource for this unit.

Heart of Wisdom Publishing   WISDOM 85

Dealing with Temptation Wisely LS10110

Step 1: Excite

Discuss and write down at least five times when you have been tempted to sin. Next to each temptation, write down where the temptation began (friends, self, TV, computer, music). John speaks of three kinds of temptations in 1 John 2:16. Can you sort the temptation you experienced into one of these categories?

1. The lust of the flesh
2. The lust of the eyes
3. The pride of life

How do you handle temptations? Have you ever been tempted beyond what you could bear? (Remember: Temptation is not sin. Jesus was tempted and never sinned. Temptation becomes sin only when the evil is accepted and yielded to.) What did you do to prevent yourself from falling for the temptation? Brainstorm and list at least three steps you have successfully used to overcome temptation.

Step 2: Examine

In the Bible, temptations are referred to as *fiery darts, thorns in the flesh, buffetings, siftings, wrestlings, combats,* all which denote hardship and suffering.

The *New Bible Dictionary* explains the difference between God's tests and Satan's temptations:

> God tests his people by putting them in situations which reveal the quality of their faith and devotion, so that all can see what is in their hearts (Gn. 22:1; Ex. 16:4, 20:20; Dt. 8:2,16, 13:3; Jdg. 2:22; 2 Ch. 32:31). By thus making trial of them, he purifies them, as metal is purified in the refiner's crucible (Ps. 66:10; Is. 48:10; Zc. 13:9; 1 Pet. 1:6f.; *cf.* Ps. 119:67,71); he strengthens their patience and matures their Christian character (Jas. 1:2ff., 12; *cf.* 1 Pet. 5:10); and he leads them into an enlarged assurance of his love for them (*cf.* Gn. 22:15ff.; Rom. 5:3ff.). Through faithfulness in times of trial men become *dokimoi,* 'approved,' in God's sight (Jas. 1:12; 1 Cor. 11:19).

> Satan tests God's people by manipulating circumstances, within the limits that God allows him (*cf.* Jb. 1:12; 2:6; 1 Cor. 10:13), in an attempt to make them desert God's will. The NT knows him as 'the tempter' (*ho peirazo_n,* Mt. 4:3; 1 Thes. 3:5), the implacable foe of both God and men (1 Pet. 5:8; Rev. 12). Christians must constantly be watchful (Mk. 14:38; Gal. 6:1; 2 Cor. 2:11) and active (Eph. 6:10ff.; Jas. 4:7; 1 Pet. 5:9) against the devil, for he is always at work trying to make them fall; whether by crushing them under the weight of hardship or pain (Jb. 1:11-2:7; 1 Pet. 5:9; Rev. 2:10; *cf.* 3:10; Heb. 2:18), or by urging them to a wrong fulfillment of natural desires (Mt. 4:3f.; 1 Cor. 7:5), or by making them complacent, careless and self-assertive (Gal. 6:1; Eph. 4:27), or by misrepresenting God to them and engendering false ideas of his truth and his will (Gn. 3:1-5; *cf.* 2 Cor. 11:3; Mt. 4:5ff.; 2 Cor. 11:14; Eph. 6:11).

Mt. 4:5. shows that Satan can even quote (and misapply) Scripture for this purpose. But God promises that a way of deliverance will always be open when he allows Satan to tempt Christians (1 Cor. 10:13; 2 Pet. 2:9; *cf.* 2 Cor. 12:7-10).

Sin in the Garden

The first temptation in the Bible was when Adam and Eve were told not to eat from the tree of the knowledge of good and evil. To keep or break this commandment was the principal means of showing obedience or disobedience to the will of God. The temptation did not come from God, but from Satan in the form of a serpent. First, Satan isolated Eve from Adam to weaken her (Heb. 10:24–25). Then he caused her to doubt God's motives (Gen. 3:4). Satan's focus was to convince Eve that God's restrictions were not good. Satan rationalized the disobedience and focused Eve's attention on desirable ends, relying on the appeal of her senses (Gen. 3:6).

Jesus Was Tempted

Immediately after His baptism, just before starting His preaching ministry, Jesus was tempted in the wilderness. Matthew 4:1–11:

> *Then was Jesus led up of the Spirit into the wilderness to be tempted of the devil. And when he had fasted forty days and forty nights, he was afterward an hungered. And when the tempter came to him, he said, If thou be the Son of God, command that these stones be made bread. But he answered and said, It is written, Man shall not live by bread alone, but by every word that proceedeth out of the mouth of God. Then the devil taketh him up into the holy city, and setteth him on a pinnacle of the temple, And saith unto him, If thou be the Son of God, cast thyself down: for it is written, He shall give his angels charge concerning thee: and in their hands they shall bear thee up, lest at any time thou dash thy foot against a stone.*

> *Jesus said unto him, It is written again, Thou shalt not tempt the Lord thy God. Again, the devil taketh him up into an exceeding high mountain, and sheweth him all the kingdoms of the world, and the glory of them; And saith unto him, All these things will I give thee, if thou wilt fall down and worship me. Then saith Jesus unto him, Get thee hence, Satan: for it is written, Thou shalt worship the Lord thy God, and him only shalt thou serve. Then the devil leaveth him, and, behold, angels came and ministered unto him.*

The temptation was not a challenge to prove that Jesus is the Son of God, but a struggle over whether he would obey God's call. In each temptation, Jesus answered the devil with Scripture. Jesus quotes the Book of Deuteronomy three times to muster spiritual support in response to the three temptations of Satan (Matt. 4:1–11).

In James chapter 1, Jesus talks about temptation:

> *Let no man say when he is tempted, I am tempted of God: for God cannot be tempted with evil, neither tempteth he any man: But every man is tempted, when he is drawn away of his own lust, and enticed. Then when lust hath conceived, it bringeth forth sin:*

Recommended in: ◆ several lessons in this unit; ♥ several HOW unit studies.   ☞ Key Resource for this unit.

and sin, when it is finished, bringeth forth death. Do not err, my beloved brethren. Every good gift and every perfect gift is from above, and cometh down from the Father of lights, with whom is no variableness, neither shadow of turning. Of his own will begat he us with the word of truth, that we should be a kind of firstfruits of his creatures. (Jas. 1:13–18)

Lead Us Not into Temptation

Jesus told us to pray, "Lead us not into temptation" in the Lord's Prayer. This phrase probably should be understood as "Do not allow us to go into temptation" (Matt. 6:13a). In the Lord's Prayer, the word *temptation* seems to be related to man's inclination to sin. To avoid sin, a person must not place himself in a position in which he will be put to the test. A tradition preserved in the Talmud is instructive: One should never put himself to the test [i.e., place himself in a tempting situation]. David the King of Israel did so and he fell. (*The Lord's Prayer "Lead Us Not Into Temptation"* by Brad Young.)

Randall Buth explains in "Deliver Us from Evil" from *Jerusalem Perspective*:

> In comparison with Luke's conclusion to the prayer, "And lead us *not into temptation*," Matthew's version more completely reflects what Jesus probably said to his disciples. Matthew's pairing of *not leading into temptation* with delivering from evil is parallelism, a hallmark of Hebrew poetry.

> Recognizing the parallelism also reinforces the correct interpretation of the verse. "Lead us not into temptation" is a Jewish way of saying "Do not let us succumb to the temptation of sin." The next line, "Deliver us from evil," conveys a similar idea. It means "Keep us from doing evil," that is, "Do not let us succumb to our evil inclination, do not let us sin." In addition, just as good poetry can convey multiple allusions, so "Deliver us from evil" can carry the additional notions of protection from evil people and evil spirits, and from trouble and calamities.

When we look at the Lord's Prayer with an understanding of its rich Jewish background, it would read more like: "Oh, Heavenly Father, lead us away from sin and restrain our evil inclination! May this include keeping us out of harm's way, and protecting us from evil!"

Resisting Temptation

We can depend on God, who is faithful, to provide us escape from any temptations. God makes available the resources necessary to resist temptation. 1 Cor. 10:13 gives us a splendid promise:

> *There hath no temptation taken you but such as is common to man: but God is faithful, who will not suffer you to be tempted above that ye are able; but will with the temptation also make a way of escape, that ye may be able to bear it.*

God gives us what we need to bear trials. He is the God of all grace who comforts us in all our afflictions.

Suggested Resources

Below are more resources on dealing with temptation wisely.

Walking Wisely ●— ◆
Chapter 5, "Wisdom for Confronting Temptation" (113–136). You will be advised to read other chapters with upcoming lessons in this book.

Additional Reading

A Way of Escape: Experiencing God's Victory over Temptation
by Jerry Newcombe, Kirsti Newcombe
Thank God that for every temptation we encounter, there's a virtue at our defense! Jerry and Kirsti Newcombe direct us to those virtues in *A Way of Escape: Experiencing God's Victory over Temptation*. Using stories from the Bible and personal experiences, the Newcombes demonstrate how subtly sin slips into our lives, and how graciously God arms us with humility, contentment, and other weapons to ward it off. Paperback - 192 pages (1999). Broadman & Holman; ISBN: 080541763X.

Personal Holiness in Times of Temptation by Bruce H. Wilkinson
Christian men face greater challenges from today's culture than simply the struggle to stay morally pure. In thirty days, you'll learn how to stick to God's standards no matter what the world throws at you. In four sessions, Dr. Bruce Wilkinson explains why holiness is not all up to God; it's also up to us. It's our job to flee temptation and learn to live a life of moral victory. Fortunately, the Scriptures are full of practical advice on how to do just that. By using this course workbook together with the video, you'll have everything you need to experience personal holiness in times of temptation. Contains: four video sessions (thirty minutes each); thirty audio devotionals; personal holiness textbook; personal holiness thirty-day workbook; "Victory Over Temptation" (resource guide with thirty articles on personal holiness). Paperback - 261 pages (August 1998). Harvest House Publishers; ISBN: 1565079434.

Internet Sources

Develop Self Control and Resist Temptation
Study is adapted from *Defeating Temptation: Biblical Secrets to Self Control* by Doug Britton.
http://www.dougbrittonbooks.com/resources/temptmakeplans010426.asp

Temptation
Fill-in-the-blanks worksheet on Temptation.
http://my.execpc.com/~combapt/tempt.html

Lead Us Not Into Temptation
A portion of the Lord's Prayer study by Brad Young.
http://articles.jerusalemperspective.com/articles/DisplayArticle.aspx?ArticleID=1532

Recommended in: ◆ several lessons in this unit; ● several HOW unit studies. ●— Key Resource for this unit.

Where He Leads, I Will Follow!
Article by Clarence H. Wagner, Jr.. Be sure to read Part 2 which includes "What About Tests And Temptations?"
http://www.bridgesforpeace.com/publications/teaching/Article-27.html

Step 3: Expand

Choose and complete one or more of the following activities:

Activity 1: Write a Summary
Read the following passages and write a one-sentence summary for each, explaining how Christians should handle temptation:

1. Resist, in faith (Eph. 6:16; 1 Pe. 5:9)
2. Watch against (Matt. 26:41; 1 Pet. 5:8)
3. Pray to be kept from (Matt. 6:13, 26:41)
4. Not to occasion, to others (Rom. 14:13)
5. Restore those overcome by (Gal. 6:1)
6. Avoid the way of (Prov. 4:14,15)

Activity 2: Make a Contrast-and-Compare Chart
Read the stories of temptation in the Bible. Make a chart comparing each temptation and how each person handled it.

1. Eve (Gen. 3:1,4,5)
2. Joseph (Gen. 39:7)
3. Achan (Josh. 7:21)
4. David (2 Sam. 11:2)
5. Peter (Mark 14:57–71)
6. Jesus (Matt. 4; Heb. 2:18, 4:15)

Activity 3: Make a Contrast-and-Compare Chart
Fill out a chart explaining some reasons temptation arises. Make three columns in your chart titled:

1. Poverty (read Prov. 30:9; Matt. 4:2,3)
2. Prosperity (read Prov. 30:9; Matt. 4:8)
3. Worldly Glory (read Num. 22:17; Dan. 4:30, 5:2; Matt. 4:8)

Activity 4: Do a Bible Study
Research and record the results of Adam's and Eve's sin. Write a one-sentence summary about each of these verses, explaining what occurred as a result of the sin:

1. Genesis 3:14
2. Genesis 15
3. Genesis 16
4. Genesis 17–19
5. Romans 5:12–21

Step 4: Excel

We who seek God's will are tempted. Our job is to work to become sanctified—set apart for God—as we become transformed in mind, heart, body, and spirit. Temptation is not just a desire, but a desire that captures us once we begin to dwell on it. Develop a plan for overcoming temptation. At the first sign of a questionable action or desire, ask the famous question, "What would Jesus do?" At the same time, have a prayer ready in your mind to say at the first sign of a desire to sin. Ask God to come to your aid to help you resist. Write such a prayer now and memorize it.

Recommended in: ◆ several lessons in this unit; ● several HOW unit studies. ◉— Key Resource for this unit.

Heart of Wisdom Publishing   WISDOM   91

Wise Relationships LS10111

Step 1: Excite

True friendships bring us cheer, approval, comfort, love, and joy. We all desire friendships. God placed this desire in you. God designed you to have a personal relationship with Him through His son, Jesus Christ. He also placed a desire in you to want close friends. Your interaction with friends is an important element of emotional and spiritual growth. Friendships can have positive and negative influences. The friendships you make when you are young establish relational skills for the future.

In the book, *Relationships: What It Takes to Be a Friend*, Pamela Reeve explains, "We need relationships to help each other do God's will. When our hearts are heavy or anxious and we are struggling to accept God's will, we need someone to pray with us and for us."

Have your friends tried to push you into things that you don't want to do or know are wrong? As challenging as these pressures may be, they are an opportunity for you to learn to stand up to things that are not right.

Old Testament Law forbade yoking a donkey and an ox as a work team (Deut. 22:10). Discuss why you think there was such a law. You'll see how this relates to friendship later in this lesson.

How many dependable, loyal relationships do you have? How did you choose each person as a friend? Brainstorm and make a list of character traits you see in your friends. Make another list of character traits you look for in finding new friends.

Step 2: Examine

Proverbs and Ecclesiastes speak of the benefits and requirements of friendship. Prov. 17:17 says *A friend loveth at all times.* One of the greatest biblical examples of the "friend who sticks closer than a brother" is the relationship between David and Jonathan. Jonathan's loyalty to David ran deeper than his loyalty to his father Saul or to his own ambitions. Read and discuss 1 Sam. 18:1–4; 20:14–17.

Abraham is called "the friend of God" (Jas. 2:23). As a result God made an "everlasting covenant" (Gn 12: 1-3, 13, 17:7, 19; 1 Ch 16:16-18; Ps 105:8-12; 118:9, etc.) that extended for all time to Abraham's descendants, the Hebrews. The promise includes:

- Blessings for those people and nations that bless Abraham and the nation that comes from him.
- Cursings upon those people and nations that curse Abraham and Israel.
- Blessings upon all the families of the earth through the Messiah, who provides salvation for the entire world.

Jesus is the ultimate friend of man. In the Gospel of John He said, *"This is my commandment, that ye love one another, as I have loved you. Greater love hath no man than this, that a man lay down his life for his friends. Ye are my friends, if ye do whatsoever I command you."* Jesus tasted death for every man and shed his blood for the remission of man's sins (Heb. 2:9; Matt. 26:28). Jesus offers man the ultimate friendship. He accepts people unconditionally. He listens and meets needs. He is faithful and He values you as a friend. If you are in need of a friend—begin with Jesus. He is your dearest friend.

Our earthly friends can bring help in time of trouble (Prov. 17:17, 27:10; Luke 11:5–8), and help us with advice in confusing situations (Prov. 27:9). Such as when Barzillai the Gileadite consoles David (2 Sam. 19:31–39), or when the friends of Jephthah's daughter help her mourn her early death (Judg. 11:37–38). A friend may offer help at the risk of death, as Hushai the Arkite does when he spies for David in the court of Absalom the usurper (2 Sam. 15:32–37; 16:16–19; 17:5–16). A friend may rebuke in love, proving more faithful than a flatterer (Prov. 27:6).

Friendship also has its dangers. Sometimes a friend can tempt you to evil, such as Judah's friend Hirah the Adullamite in Genesis 38:12–23, or Jonadab son of Shimeah in 2 Samuel 13:1–6. A wise relationship will refuse to be linked with evil. Commitment to Christ calls for purification "from everything that contaminates body and spirit"(2 Cor. 7:1).

The Bible is clear that we must be especially careful in choosing our friends. *The righteous is more excellent than his neighbour: but the way of the wicked seduceth them* (Prov. 12:26). *He who walks with wise men will be wise, but the companion of fools will be destroyed* (Prov. 13:20). Friendships that are based on money (Prov. 6:1–5, 14:20, 19:4,6–7) or sin (Prov. 16:29–30, 1:10–19) are destined to be disappointing. So are friendships with people who have bad tempers (Prov. 22:24–25), who speak foolishly (Prov. 14:7), who rebel against authority (Prov. 24:21–22, NIV), or who are dishonest (Prov. 29:27). *Blessed is the man that walketh not in the counsel of the ungodly, nor standeth in the way of sinners, nor sitteth in the seat of the scornful* (Ps. 1:1–2).

To choose friends wisely, you must pray for discernment (Gen. 41:33, 39; 1 Kings 3:12; 2 Chr. 2:12; Prov. 10:13, 14:33, 16:21, 17:24,28) and ask your parents for advice.

Paul's urgent appeal not to be "unequally yoked" with unbelievers is an image from the Old Testament Law which forbade yoking a donkey and an ox as a work team (Deut. 22:10).

> *Be ye not unequally yoked together with unbelievers: for what fellowship hath right-eousness with unrighteousness? and what communion hath light with darkness?* [15] *And what concord hath Christ with Belial? or what part hath he that believeth with an infi-del?* [16] *And what agreement hath the temple of God with idols? for ye are the temple of the living God; as God hath said, I will dwell in them, and walk in them; and I will be their God, and they shall be my people.* [17] *Wherefore come out from among them, and be ye separate, saith the Lord, and touch not the unclean thing; and I will receive you, And will be a Father unto you, and ye shall be my sons and daughters, saith the Lord Almighty.* (2 Cor. 6:14–18)

Recommended in: ◆ several lessons in this unit; ❤ several HOW unit studies. ☛ Key Resource for this unit.

Suggested Resources

Below are more resources about wise relationships:

 *Our Father Abraham: Jewish Roots of the Christian Faith* ◆
"Marriage and the Family Through Hebrew Eyes" (195–236)

Walking Wisely ⊙— ◆
Chapter 6, "Wisdom in Choosing Friends and Business Associates" (139–156) and Chapter 7, "Wisdom for Building Deep, Lasting, Godly Friendships" (159–182). You will be advised to read other chapters with upcoming lessons in this book.

Additional Reading

 *Faithfulness: The Foundation of True Friendship* by Jacalyn Eyre
We all need faithful friends—people who accept us as we are, who seek our best interests, and who stick with us in crisis. Yet being a faithful friend is more important than finding one. This Fruit of the Spirit Bible study looks at sixteen essential qualities we need to become faithful friends. These qualities help us lay a foundation for lasting relationships. Designed for use in small groups or personal devotions, the interactive format will help you grow in your ability to reflect the character of Jesus. Six lessons are included, with leader's notes. Paperback - 80 pages (2001). Zondervan; ISBN: 0310238633.

 *Friendship Factor: How to Get Closer to the People You Care For* by Alan Loy McGinnis
Some people have countless friends—what's their secret? How can I get close and stay close to people I like? What's the key to a successful marriage? Alan Loy McGinnis, pastor and counselor, answers these and many more questions concerning the all-important topic of human relationships. Through the use of captivating case histories and anecdotes about such famous people as George Burns, Howard Hughes, Helen Keller, and C.S. Lewis, McGinnis shares the secret of how to love and be loved. Paperback - 192 pages (May 1979). Augsburg Fortress Publishers; ISBN: 080661711X.

 Friendship: Portraits in God's Family Album (Fisherman Bible Studies) by Steve Brestin
The Bible abounds with stories of deep and lasting friendship, portraits of characters in God's family. This study offers insights for better, more meaningful friendships by examining historical models, including Abraham, Ruth, David and Jonathan, Mary and Elizabeth, Jesus, and Barnabas. The characteristics of commitment, unfailing kindness, and open sharing are repeated. Jesus is reflected in the faces of historical models, the One who models each of these characteristics perfectly. Fisherman Bible Studies are among the most popular on the market. There are nearly sixty book, character, topical, or core studies to choose from, so you're bound to find something just right for your group. Each study features built-in leadership

helps and a flexible format which you can use in all kinds of settings. Eleven studies for individuals or groups. Paperback - 80 pages (July 1999). Harold Shaw Publishers; ISBN: 0877882878.

 *Relationships: What It Takes to Be a Friend* by Pamela Reeve
Explains how to make good relationships and how to avoid the pitfalls. This book incorporates life-changing principles needed to build and maintain healthy relationships. Hardcover - 96 pages (February 1997). Multnomah Publishers Inc.; ISBN: 1576730441.

Audio

Building Wise Relationships by Charles Stanley
David and Jonathan; Paul and Timothy. A true friend can accept the worst about you and still help you become your very best. In this three-tape audio series, Dr. Stanley describes relationships to avoid while he teaches that it takes sacrifice, time, and transparency to build deep, significant relationships. Series of three audio tapes. Available from In Touch Ministries: http://Intouch.org or (800) 789-1473.

Internet Sources

How to Be God's Friend
Article on Crosswalk.com
http://www.crosswalk.com/faith/ministry_articles/1192860.html

How to Find True Friends
Article from eharmony.com
http://www.crosswalk.com/community/singles/1164812.html

Friendship
A Bible study worksheet on friendship.
http://my.execpc.com/~combapt/friends.html

Step 3: Expand

Choose and complete one or more of the following activities:

Activity 1: Make a List
Make a list of statements about friendship from *Walking Wisely* by Charles Stanley, Chapter 6 (139–156). Examples: "A friend can drive you to excellence because..." or, "A friendship can drag you down because... " or "We should avoid the person that is rebellious because..."

Activity 2: Outline
Outline Chapter 7 of *Walking Wisely* by Charles Stanley. Write a summary paragraph for each of the Eight Steps to Building Wise Relationships.

1. Share concerns and interests
2. Focus on meeting another's needs and not yours

Recommended in: ◆ several lessons in this unit; ♥ several HOW unit studies. ☞ Key Resource for this unit.

3. Risk rejection and pain
4. Love sacrificially
5. Be open and transparent
6. Ask for forgiveness and be willing to accept forgiveness
7. Accept criticism and praise
8. Allow biblical principles to govern your relationship

Activity 3: Perform a Skit
King Saul's oldest son Jonathan stripped himself of his royal ceremonial dress and placed it on David in recognition of David's divine election to be king (1 Sam. 18:4; cf. 23:17). The covenant of friendship between the two men is documented in the Bible. 1 Samuel says that *the soul of Jonathan was knit to the soul of David.* Read about David and Jonathan in 1 Sam. 18:1–4; 20; 23:16–18; 2 Sam. 1:17–27; 9:1–13. Write and perform a skit about their relationship for your family.

Activity 4: Dig Deeper
In 2 Cor. 6:14–18, the appeal to *not be yoked together with unbelievers* means here not participating in pagan worship with unbelievers. This is made clear by the series of five rhetorical questions which follow in vv. 14b–16, especially the last one: *What agreement is there between the temple of God and idols?* (16b). Believers cannot participate in idolatrous worship because they are *the temple of the living God,* and God has said, *"I will live with them and walk among them."* Because a person cannot both walk with God and participate in idolatrous worship, believers must separate themselves from idolatry. Paul stresses this by appealing to OT calls to have nothing to do with what is *unclean* and OT promises of God to welcome as a Father those who turn from idolatry (17–18). In the light of these promises, Paul urges his readers to leave behind everything that contaminates and to concentrate on *perfecting holiness out of reverence for God* (2 Cor. 7:1). In Paul's time pagan worship was obvious. Think about and discuss what *pagan* means today. What are some pagan activities we should avoid?

Activity 5: Copy Passages
Copy at least five Bible passages or make a table of passages explaining how to identify people with true wisdom: Behavior (Prov. 10:23), good deeds and humility (Jas. 3:13), and what comes from the mouth (Ps. 36:3; Ps. 49:3; Prov. 10:13–14,19,31; Prov. 14:3; Prov. 15:2,7; Prov. 16:23; Prov. 17:28; Prov. 18:4; Eccl. 10:12) are indicators of the presence or absence of wisdom. A wise person fears God's name (Mic. 6:9), and obeys God (Matt. 7:24). Those who are wise bring joy to parents and leaders (Prov. 10:1; Prov. 14:35; Prov. 15:20; Prov. 23:24; Prov. 27:11; Prov. 29:3). A wise person listens to advice and instruction (Prov. 12:15; Prov. 13:1,10; Prov. 15:12,31; Prov. 19:20; Prov. 21:11; Prov. 25:12; Prov. 29:15; Eccl. 7:5; Eccl. 9:17) and stores up knowledge (Prov. 10:14; Prov. 18:15; Prov. 23:23). One with wisdom is wise about what is good (Rom. 16:19) and shuns evil (Prov. 3:7; Prov. 10:23; Prov. 14:16; Rom. 16:19). He is not led astray by wine or beer (Prov. 20:1), he shows restraint in the pursuit of riches (Prov. 23:4), and he keeps his anger under control (Prov. 29:11). One who is wise does not compare himself with or measure himself by others (2 Cor. 10:12), and he does not show partiality in judging (Prov. 24:23). A wise person does not boast of wisdom (Jer. 9:23) but is praised according to his wisdom (Prov. 12:8) and inherits honor (Prov. 3:35).

Activity 6 Make a List
Why does a friendship last or end? Make a list of benefits of friendship using the following verses: Prov. 27:6,7,10, and 17:17.

Activity 7: Make a Contrast-and-Compare Chart
Look up two or three passages about friendships from the list below. Contrast and compare the chosen passages in a contrast-and-compare chart. *(a)* Abraham and Lot, Gen. 14:14–16; *(b)* Ruth and Naomi, Ruth 1:16,17; *(c)* Samuel and Saul, 1 Sam. 15:35; 16:1; *(d)* David and Jonathan, 1 Sam. 18:14; 20; 23:16–18; 2 Sam. 1:17–27; 9:1–13; *(e)* David and Abiathar, 1 Sam. 22:23; *(f)* David and Nahash, 2 Sam. 10:2; *(g)* David and Hiram, 1 Kings 5:1; *(h)* David and Mephibosheth, 2 Sam. 9; *(i)* David and Hushai, 2 Sam. 15:32–37; 16; 17:1–22; *(j)* David and Ittai, 2 Sam. 15:19–21; *(k)* Joram and Ahaziah, 2 Kings 8:28,29; 9:16; *(l)* Jehu and Jehonadab, 2 Kings 10:15–27; *(m)* Job and his three friends, Job 2:11–13; *(n)* Daniel and his three companions, Dan. 2:49; *(o)* Mary, Martha, Lazarus, and Jesus, Luke 10:38–42; John 11:1–46; *(p)* The Marys, Joseph of Arimathea, and Jesus, Matt. 27:55–61; 28:1–8; Luke 24:10; John 20:11–18; *(q)* Luke and Theophilus, Acts 1:1; *(r)* Paul and his nephew, Acts 23:16; *(s)* Paul, Priscilla, and Aquila, Rom. 16:3,4; *(t)* Paul, Timothy, and Epaphroditus, Phil. 2:19,20,22,25. Refer to http://HeartofWisdom.com/Worksheets.htm

Activity 8: Write a Poem
Write a memory poem about friendship. Follow one of the three traditional forms: Ballad, blank verse or Haiku (explained in "Related Forms," *Writers INC.*) Follow the steps for searching, selecting, generating, writing, revising, and evaluating in "Writing Poetry" in *Writers INC* (includes a sample memory poem).

The New International Version	American Standard Version	Today's English Version	The New Century Version	The New Living Translation
Be very careful, then, how you live—not as unwise but as wise, making the most of every opportunity, because the days are evil. Therefore do not be foolish, but understand what the Lord's will is.	Look therefore carefully how ye walk, not as unwise, but as wise; redeeming the time, because the days are evil. Wherefore be ye not foolish, but understand what the will of the Lord is.	So be careful how you live. Don't live like ignorant people, but like wise people. Make good use of every opportunity you have, because these are evil days. Don't be fools, then, but try to find out what the Lord wants you to do.	So be very careful how you live. Do not live like those who are not wise, but live wisely. Use every chance you have for doing good, because these are evil times. So do not be foolish but learn what the Lord wants you to do.	So be careful how you live, not as fools but as those who are wise. Make the most of every opportunity for doing good in these evil days. Don't act thoughtlessly, but try to understand what the Lord wants you to do.

Recommended in: ◆ several lessons in this unit; ● several HOW unit studies. ☛ Key Resource for this unit.

Step 4: Excel

Share at least one good thing that has resulted in your life from a good friendship. Then share at least one bad result in your life from a negative friendship. Are there more negative than positive results or vice versa? Discuss why this might be. Should you reevaluate your relationships? Do you think it is justifiable to have a negative friendship if your only other option is not having a friend? Ask yourself why you choose the friends you do. Do you feel it is necessary to have friends your own age? Do you consider your family members as your friends?

What kind of friend are you? Have you been a positive influence on your friends? Do they look to you for encouragement and advice? Do your friends trust you with their dreams and disappointments? Do you do most of the talking or most of the listening? Would your friends describe you as faithful? Do you share God's Word with them? Do you pray for and with them?

If you aren't happy with the answers to these questions, you should study the meaning of true friendship by reading one or more of the books listed in step 2.

Wise Goal-Setting LS10112

Step 1: Excite

Are you happy with who, what, and where you are today? Are you having fun? Are you enjoying your school work? Your relationships? If you don't like where you are today, then don't expect tomorrow to be any different without change. You may need to make changes by changing your attitude, your priorities, and/or your activities.

Brainstorm and discuss the importance of goal-setting. Why should you set goals? Should goals be clearly defined? Will a set of goals increase your motivation to achieve? Can goal-setting help you concentrate better? Can setting goals cause or prevent stress and anxiety? Will goal-setting improve self-discipline? Can goals help you concentrate on and improve in spiritual areas?

As you work through this lesson, honestly evaluate yourself in the area of goal-setting. If you find yourself lacking, determine to become a goal-setter.

Step 2: Examine

Only God knows His plans for your life. Jer. 29:11 says, *For I know the plans I have for you, declares the LORD, plans to prosper you and not to harm you, plans to give you hope and a future.* However, you can prayerfully set your own goals. Goals help you decide what is important for you to achieve in your life. They separate the important from the irrelevant. They motivate you. Goals have a clear-cut outcome. Your main goal now may be to graduate; this is considered a short-term goal. You should also have life goals, such as marriage and having a family. In each case, you have something specific and concrete to look forward to and work toward.

> *The steps of a good man are ordered by the LORD:*
> *and he delighteth in his way.* (Ps. 37:23)

Goals are not wishes or dreams. Wishes and dreams are wants and desires which we hope will materialize. Goals are things we desire that we actually work toward, usually with a date. Research has shown that people who write down their goals and make lists of things to do generally achieve their goals. By knowing exactly what you want to achieve, you know what you need to concentrate on and improve.

> When we set goals we are in command. If we know where we are going, we can judge more accurately where we are now and make effective plans to reach our destination. If we keep a goal firmly in mind, we will know when we have reached it. This gives us a sense of accomplishment and the challenge of establishing fresh, new goals—always keeping the long-range objective in mind. If we can state our goals clearly, we will gain a purpose and meaning in all our actions. Clearly understood goals bring our lives into focus just as a magnifying glass focuses a beam of light into one burning point. Without goals our efforts may be scattered and unproductive. Without knowing it, we may be torn by conflicting impulses or desires. (President Ezra Taft Benson, 27 June 1974. *Mission Presidents Seminar*, SLC; see *TETB* 384)

Recommended in: ◆ several lessons in this unit; ❤ several HOW unit studies. ◉— Key Resource for this unit.

Goal-setting gives you both long-term vision and short-term motivation. When you make a list of goals, it will help you see, understand, and organize your resources and arrange the steps needed to pursue your goals. By setting clearly defined goals, you can measure your achievement. You can see progress. Through achieving your goals, you will become more disciplined in life. Remember that the goal of accomplishing God's will should always be before you.

But they that wait upon the LORD shall renew their strength; they shall mount up with wings as eagles; they shall run, and not be weary; and they shall walk, and not faint. (Isaiah 40:31)

Do not lay up for yourselves treasures upon earth, where moth and rust destroy, and where thieves break in and steal. But lay up for yourselves treasures in heaven, where neither moth nor rust destroys, and where thieves do not break in and steal. (Matt. 6:19–20)

We should aim for high goals. They should be challenging. M. Grinard wrote about a plant which germinated in the bottom of a mine and raised itself to the height of one hundred and twenty feet in order to reach the light, though the usual height of this particular plant is only six inches.[1] This does not mean, however, that we should set unrealistic goals.

A wise person will always have a goal that they are pushing toward. As Christians we should all have the ultimate goal of becoming what God has purposed us to be in this life. Phil. 3:14 says it this way: *I press toward the goal for the prize of the upward call of God in Christ Jesus.* That is a goal we can all set.

We are accountable for our time on earth. Setting goals will help us use our time constructively. Eph. 5:15–17 says: *See then that ye walk circumspectly, not as fools, but as wise, Redeeming the time, because the days are evil. Wherefore be ye not unwise, but understanding what the will of the Lord is.* Read this passage in other versions of the Bible:

Our goals must be made in the light of God's Word and with the prerequisite "If the Lord wills," we will do this or that. Our dealings must be done with full conviction; otherwise, we will miss the mark.

> Usually the Lord gives us the overall objectives to be accomplished and some guidelines to follow, but He expects us to work out most of the details and methods. The methods and procedures are usually developed through study and prayer and by living so that we can obtain and follow the promptings of the Spirit. Less spiritually advanced people, such as those in the days of Moses, had to be commanded in many things. Today those spiritually alert look at the objectives, check the guidelines laid down by the Lord and His prophets, and then prayerfully act—without having to be commanded "in all things" (D&C 58:26). This attitude prepares men for godhood. (President Ezra Taft Benson, *An Enemy Hath Done This*, pp. 271–272)

Goal Guidelines:

Make your goals specific. Having a vague goal is not much better than having no goal at all. A vague goal would be "to become a better Christian." A specific goal would be "to read my Bible thirty minutes a day."

Make your goals attainable. If one of your goals is to lose weight, it should be attainable and realistic. Losing thirty pounds in a month is unrealistic. Losing a pound a week is attainable.

Focus first on the goals that matter. To accomplish primary goals, you will often need to put equally desirable but less important ones on a back burner.

Monitor progress periodically. Assess your goals on a regular basis; revise the objectives, tactics, and strategy to achieve each goal without changing it.

Adjust your goals as you need to. If one of your goals is to exercise three days a week but you have a physical setback, you might have to limit your time exercising until you are more fit.

Include your parents. Make sure your parents are a part of the goal-setting process. Brothers and sisters should have some say in goals that affect them.

Starting something new will be very exciting. Everything related to your goals can be interesting. During your goal-setting journey you'll be studying and seeking the counsel of others. Goal-setting means you might lie awake at night, solving problems, calculating costs, and figuring out how you will overcome obstacles. Your planning should be in writing so that you can keep track of what you are learning. Accomplishing goals will usually create a need for continuous maintenance. Remember that we reap what we sow. If you set your goals carefully now, you will have less regret when you are an adult.

There will be times of setbacks. Waiting for God's timing requires trust and faith. God denies us good things in the present only because He has something better for us in the future.

Suggested Resources

Below are more resources on goal-setting:

Reaching Your Full Potential: Simple Steps to Achieving Your Goals
by Richard Furman
Faced with the grueling demands of training to be a surgeon, Dr. Richard Furman realized that the key to survival and success would be to set clear goals and create specific steps for reaching them. These simple, easy-to-remember guidelines can be applied to any pursuit in life and powerfully affirm the most important goal in life—to live for God and glorify Him. Paperback - 240 pages (2001). Harvest House Publishers; ISBN: 0736907130.

Audio

Go for Your Goals—Audio book by Michael Podolinsky
When you tap into the power of effective goals, nothing can hold you back! So, why not do it now? In less than two hours, you'll have everything you need to create a winning career plan, rewarding relationships, and a terrific future. It's surprisingly easy to reach your goals—once you know the secrets. You'll learn the five essential parts of any goal, what happens when one part is missing, how to choose goals that really motivate you, and how to keep yourself on track to achieve them. Waiting inside this book is the support you need— the encouragement to "aim high," the motivation to stay on target, and the support to pull

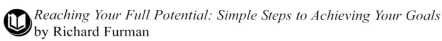

Recommended in: ◆ several lessons in this unit; ❤ several HOW unit studies. ☛ Key Resource for this unit.

Heart of Wisdom Publishing   WISDOM 101

you through when times get tough. You'll learn tricks that power-pack your time, double your productivity, and help you reach every goal faster. One pocket guide. Two cassettes. Also available on CD. (1995). Oasis Audio; ISBN: 1556780567.

Software

GoalPro 5.0
This software provides all the necessary tools to maintain an efficient and effective goal-setting routine. It provides you with an innovative system for breaking down your larger goals into smaller, more focused, supporting goals, to even smaller time-scheduled tasks and appointments. You will develop the daily confidence of knowing that simply performing the day's scheduled events will, over time, lead to the achievement of your much larger goals. Order at http://www.goalpro.com.

Internet Sources

About Goal Setting
Outlines a seven-step process for getting motivated, setting goals, and achieving success. Links to goal-setting software and audio courses. http://www.about-goal-setting.com/

Christian Goal Setting and Achieving
Christian goal-setting and achieving course and software; Christian training events; "Examine Yourself" and "DISCover Yourself" lifestyle, character, and personality profiles; financial accounting.
http://www.christiangoalsetting.com/

MyMotivator.com
Free goal-setting software and on-demand, streaming RealAudio and RealVideo motivational and inspirational audio tapes. Also includes motivational and inspirational electronic postcards.
http://www.mymotivator.com/

Redeeming the Time: A Christian Perspective on Time Management
Article by Gregg Harris, home-schooling speaker and author.
http://homeschool.crosswalk.com/partner/Article_Display_Page/0,,PTID74453%7CCHID20 6826%7CCIID512660,00.html

Step 3: Expand

Complete activity 1 and any other activities you choose:

Activity 1: Set Goals

First, pray about your goals. The most important part of your planning should be spending time in prayer. Brainstorm and list several short- and long-term goals. Don't let fear of failure stop you from writing them down. The Bible says in Hab. 2:2: . . . *Write the vision and make it plain on tablets, that he may run who reads it.*

Right now you are just brainstorming, but even so, writing down your goals and/or your vision is important. It can help to keep you focused in difficult or lean times.

Make goal categories in an outline or mind map:

1. Spiritual (Bible study, prayer, courses, books to read, etc.)
2. Physical (exercise, diet, join a team, etc.)
3. Educational (classes to complete, books to read, college, training, etc.)
4. Personal Issues (habits or emotional issues that need work; getting organized, etc.)
5. Financial (saving for college, etc.)

Answer each of the following as specifically as possible:

1. What are your lifetime goals?
2. What are your goals for the next three to five years?
3. What are your goals for this year?
4. What are the things you need to do in order to accomplish this year's goals?

Next, answer these questions:

1. What skills do I currently have, how useful or marketable are they, and which new skills do I need to develop? What knowledge do I need to acquire?
2. Will my current attitudes enable me to achieve my goals?
3. To what degree will my family and friends support me in reaching my goals?
4. Whom do I know who can assist me?

Now, prioritize your list of goals. For each item on your list, ask yourself: "Is this taking me nearer to my primary goals—or leading me farther away from them?" Identify your goals clearly and decide which ones are most important—by concentrating your efforts, you have a better chance of achieving what matters most.

Next, list the things you will do this week and the things you will do today that relate to your goals for this year. As you walk through this, remember that you may alter your goals, and that's okay. Don't think that writing these things down will lock you into any specific course of action; rather, it will give you an initial direction to get started in a life of goal-setting.

Begin to keep a goal diary in which you "write the vision." Use a daily planner, notebook, or your computer (and be sure to make a back-up disk). Record the date that goals were set and met. Record *how* they were met. Also record any changes that you made in your goals.

Recommended in: ◆ several lessons in this unit; ♥ several HOW unit studies.   ☞ Key Resource for this unit.

Why did you change the original plan? How will this change affect other goals? Be as detailed as possible with this diary. It may serve as a great source of joy and encouragement in years to come.

Activity 2: Copy Quotes
It helps to look for sources of wisdom when we wish to attain goals. As we struggle to achieve our goals, we may often meet with resistance and feel like giving up. During those times, it helps to draw from a fresh well of inspiration. We can turn to quotations such as Elbert Hubbard's "God will not look you over for medals, degrees, or diplomas, but for scars." Copy quotations from this lesson or go to the library and check out one or two books of quotations (or do an Internet search). Select three suitable quotations for each of the following categories: nurturing, goal setting, reflecting, inventing, patience, and success. Choose one or two of these quotes that really inspire you and post them in visible places around your bedroom or bathroom. Draw motivation from them as you read them each day.

Activity 3: Copy Bible Passages
Copy all the Bible passages in this lesson into your portfolio. Memorize Phil. 3:14. Meditate on it as you set a time frame for your goals.

Activity 4: Conduct an Interview
Interview someone who you feel is successful in managing their time. Ask them if they write their goals down. How often? How do they set their goals? How do they keep track of accomplished goals?

Activity 5: Teach a Child
Encourage a younger child to make a commitment. Give them a one-month calendar with a square to represent each day. Let the child pick one task he or she needs to do faithfully (perhaps study, pray, a household chore, etc.). Help them check their progress at least once a week by giving them a sticker for each goal they have accomplished. Reflect on whether you think writing down their goals helped them.

Step 4: Excel

Goals should cover a sensible amount of time. Having a definite time in which to accomplish your goal helps you focus on what you should do today to progress toward that goal. For example, knowing that you have a graduation date in mind helps you to plan the units you will do now to reach that goal. Take your list of short-term and long-term goals and designate a time span for each one. Share your goals with your parents. Ask for their opinion of areas in which you could improve.

Wisdom Literature LS10113

Step 1: Excite

There are several well-known American sayings in our culture that pass on morsels of wisdom about life, such as:

- A penny saved is a penny earned
- Look before you leap
- People who live in glass houses shouldn't throw stones
- A bird in the hand is worth two in the bush

The biblical Hebrews also had proverbs to live by. The Hebrews categorized five books of the Bible as "wisdom literature" or "wisdom writings." Before you begin this lesson, brainstorm and guess which books these might be and why.

Step 2: Examine

"Wisdom literature" or "wisdom writings" are instructive forms of religious writings, demonstrated in certain books in the Old Testament. Wisdom literature is frequently cast as advice given by a father to his son, or an older man to his students (Richards, L. 1991). The wisdom literature contained in the Bible differs from that produced by other nations because it recognizes that a relationship with the Living God is the starting point in the search for wisdom (Ps.111:10; Prov. 1:7; 2:1–4; 9:10; Job 28:28; Eccl. 12:13).

The "wisdom" books of the Bible are Job, Ecclesiastes, Proverbs, and the Song of Solomon. Wisdom sayings are also found in the Psalms and in both narrative and prophecy (1 Sam. 24:13; 1 Kings 20:11; Jer. 31:29; Ezek. 18:2). In the New Testament, wisdom sayings can be found in Rom. 12; 1 Cor. 13; Gal. 5:19–23; Eph. 5:22–6:9; Col. 3:5–17; Heb. 3:12–19; 4:11–13; 6:1–12; Jas. 1v3; and 1 Pet. 2:11–17. The aim of wisdom sayings is powerfully practical, to supply you with the information you need to make the right choices.

The Wisdom Literature and Psalms by James Smith is an excellent book on this topic. Below is a summary about each book classified as wisdom literature. See the book by Smith for fascinating details.

> The poetic books have certain characteristics which set them apart from the other books of the Bible. First, these books are almost entirely written in Hebrew poetry. Second, they are not historically oriented. Except for the Book of Psalms, there are few historical allusions here. Third, these books deal with issues which are of universal concern to mankind. From the dawn of history human minds have grappled with such issues as suffering, love, and the brevity and meaning of human life. Fourth, direct divine speech is rare here. As a rule the writers are speaking for man to God rather than the reverse

---

Recommended in: ◆ several lessons in this unit; ♥ several HOW unit studies. ☛ Key Resource for this unit.

Heart of Wisdom Publishing   WISDOM 105

which is the essential characteristic of the prophetic books. Fifth, in treating these difficult topics these books exhibit boldness and honesty. Thus one could list a courageous spirit as one of the characteristics of this literature.

Job: Perhaps the Book of Job is the best known of the sacred sixty-six in circles outside the immediate company of believers. Few other compositions have such power to stretch minds, evoke sympathy, provoke inquiry, and expand vision. One who has eavesdropped on the discussions in the heavenly court, visited Job at the city dump, weighed the arguments of Job and his friends, and cowered before the thundering barrage of questions from the God of the whirlwind can never be the same again. The book contains 10,102 words organized into forty-two chapters and 1,070 verses. The book is very moving, but it is incredibly complex. It is one of the most difficult books in the Bible to translate and interpret.

Proverbs: Proverbs has its own special niche in the sacred canon. Proverbs does not allude to Israel's past or its popular heroes. Proverbs has nothing to say of Israel's fate, good or bad. Prudent and moral behavior is the concern of Proverbs; it is God's how-to-do-it manual. It teaches the skill of getting along sensibly in life while at the same time pleasing God. This book of 15,043 words is organized into thirty-one chapters, 915 verses.

Psalms: The Book of Psalms is the largest book in the Bible. The 150 psalms which constitute this book are organized into 2,461 verses. The book contains 43,743 words. This book is unique in ancient literature. Although a variety of hymns from Egypt and Mesopotamia have been preserved, no comparable collection of songs from biblical times has come to light.

Ecclesiastes: Biblical faith does not try to stifle tough questions. Experience demonstrates that doubt drives an intellectually honest person to investigation, and investigation leads to greater faith. Christianity is a thinking person's religion. Ecclesiastes may serve as a stepping stone to those who find biblical faith to be intellectually unacceptable. Ecclesiastes contains twelve chapters, 222 verses and 5,584 words. In the case of this particular book there is evidence that the original was organized into verses.

Song of Songs: If Psalms is worship literature, and Job, Proverbs and Ecclesiastes are wisdom literature, what is the Song of Songs? It offers no direct instruction, or debate. Some think it is in a category all its own, perhaps to be designated "wedding literature." In recent years, however, scholars have begun to recognize this book as a further example of wisdom literature. Love is the most essential and basic basic human experience, and human experience is what wisdom literature is all about. Like Proverbs this book does not speak of Israel's unique relationship with Yahweh. Yet this book of eight chapters (117 verses; 2,661 words) celebrates one of God's greatest gifts to man: human sexuality.

The best-known form of wisdom literature is the proverb (also called a *mashal*), which is a statement of truth expressed in few words in such a way as to hold attention. The Book of Proverbs deals with the issues that touch the individual's life, such as personal industry, integrity, sexual purity, and family relations. Hebrew poetry was based on parallelism of thought. There are four types of proverbs: comparison, antithetical, synonymous, and synthetic, and in each one the second line contains the key to understanding the proverb.

Comparison proverb: The second line draws a comparison between some basic truth and an illustration. For example:

> *As cold waters to a thirsty soul, so is good news from a far country.* (25:25)

> *Better is a dry morsel with quietness, Than a house full of feasting with strife.* (17:1)

Antithetical proverb: The second line states the same principle as the first, only from the opposite standpoint. For example:

> *A merry heart doeth good like a medicine: but a broken spirit drieth the bones.* (17:22)

Synonymous proverb: two lines, phrases, or sentences that say the same thing. For example:

> *Judgments are prepared for scorners, and stripes for the back of fools.* (19:29)

Synthetic proverb: The second line amplifies and expands the meaning of the first. For example:

> *The name of the LORD is a strong tower: the righteous runneth into it, and is safe.* (18:10)

In other wisdom books, riddles are used. See Judg. 14:12 and 1 Kings 10:1.

In the New Testament, Jesus used the teaching methods of parables and proverbs. The idea of a proverb (mashal) is to bring one thing alongside another in order to force comparison. The student moves from something well known to something less known or even unknown. The parables of Jesus are *meshalim*. The forced comparison brings light into darkness. By contrast, we could approach the subject of the human mind analytically; Jesus spoke to fishermen, farmers, and shepherds using parables about fishing, farming, and shepherding.

The Book of James also incorporates wisdom elements (see 1:5; 3:13). The Beatitudes (Matt. 5:3–12) are also in a category akin to wisdom.

Do research to find wisdom literature. Use the Bible Study Aids in the Research Area http://homeschoolunitstudies.com/Research.html or another resource (an encyclopedia, a fiction book, a historical novel, or the Internet). We recommend any of the following:

Recommended in: ◆ several lessons in this unit; ♥ several HOW unit studies. ◉➞ Key Resource for this unit.

Suggested Resources

Our Father Abraham: Jewish Roots of the Christian Faith ♥
"Wisdom Literature" (282–287; also see 10).

Additional Reading

Gospel and Wisdom: Israel's Wisdom Literature in the Christian Life by Graeme Goldsworthy
Neglected in today's climate, wisdom is a significant concept in both the Old and New Testaments. Applying the method of biblical theology, the author aims to place wisdom literature in its Christian context, firm in his conviction that wisdom is a key dimension of the Christian life and finds its center in the person of Christ. Paperback - 202 pages (1987) Paternoster Publishing; ISBN: 0853646511.

Proverbial Wisdom and Common Sense: A Messianic Jewish Approach to Today's Issues from the Proverbs by Derek Leman
People everywhere are looking for solutions to everyday problems. Yet the Bible is filled with wisdom and dedicated to the principles that can help you meet life's challenges... if only it were accessible, understandable, and usable. This book makes the *Mishlei* (the Hebrew word for the Book of Proverbs) an uncovered treasure. It also provides the New Testament references to Proverbs' principles, tying everything together. "Combines the insights gleaned from academic study with down-to-earth challenges that stimulate people to godly living...a gold mine of provocative studies." —Dr. John Walton, professor of Bible Studies, Moody Bible Institute. Chapters include: "Adonai and Wisdom"; "Some Wisdom Don'ts"; "Finances"; "Discipline and Reproof"; "Family Relationships"; "Anger and Strife." Also includes a ten-minute-a-day devotional plan. Paperback - 248 pages (July 1999) Messianic Jewish Alliance; ISBN: 1880226782.

The Wisdom Literature and Psalms by James Smith
This book explains the poetic books' characteristics which set them apart from the other books of the Bible. It describes how this literature speaks to human minds grappling with such issues as suffering, love, and the brevity and meaning of human life. Hardcover - 873 pages (1987) College Press Publishing Company, Inc.; ISBN: 0899004393.

Internet Sources

Interpreting the Biblical Wisdom Literature
A precise summary of each book of wisdom literature by Robert I. Bradshaw.
http://www.robibrad.demon.co.uk/Wisdom.htm

Progression and Character of Wisdom Literature
A list of the categories of wisdom literature in chronological order.
http://www.wlu.ca/~wwwaar/syllabi/rennie/rel151/wisdom.htm

ⓘ *The Psalms and Writings*
Definition of "wisdom literature."
http://bibletutor.luthersem.edu/books/psalwisd.htm

Step 3: Expand

Complete activity 1 and one other activity listed below:

Activity 1: Create an Outline
Outline one or more books of the wisdom literature genre.

If you select **Job**, answer these questions: Is Job an historical book? Did the author intend this book to be an historical record of an actual event in the past and, if so, how precise did he intend it to be? (J. Smith)

If you select the **Psalms**, you have chosen the Hebrew prayer book. Your prayer life should be greatly enhanced.

If you select **Proverbs**, you won't be sorry. Proverbs concentrates on our daily concerns more than any other book in the Bible. You may want to try a topical outline instead of a chapter outline. *The Narrated Bible* presents Proverbs topically; use it as a guide.

If you select **Ecclesiastes**, notice the three key phrases: 1) "under the sun" (appears twenty-nine times); 2) "I thought in my heart" or "I thought to myself" (appears seven times); and 3) "vanity," or "meaningless," or "emptiness" (appears thirty-four times).

If you select the **Song of Songs**, ask your parents if they want you to outline this book before you begin. Cole said, "The Song has been described as 'a hymn in praise of sensual love with no minor strains of prudery or shame to mar its melody.'" Your parents can judge whether you are ready for this study.

Activity 2: Copy Proverbs
Look through the Book of Proverbs and write down three examples of each type of proverb: comparison, antithetical, synonymous, and synthetic.

Activity 3: Study Wisdom Literature
Read as much of the books of Proverbs/Job/Ecclesiastes as you can in one sitting, taking (mental) notes as you read. Consider what you think the central message of the text is. Ask yourself: What advice is given? What warnings are given? What comparisons are made? Compare the proverb you are reading with other similar or related proverbs (use a topical Bible to find related verses). How do the proverbs differ? If two proverbs say the opposite thing, why would this be? Do you think the statement made or the advice given is

---

Recommended in: ◆ several lessons in this unit; ♥ several HOW unit studies. ☛ Key Resource for this unit.

good? Why or why not? You must also remember that proverbs are not always globally applicable to every person and every situation. They are guidelines and "rules of thumb," not absolute rules, statements of fact, or direct promises.

Activity 4: Study Proverbs

Many proverbs deal with harvest time. Harvest in ancient Israel occurred twice a year, first as a barley harvest in the valleys, then in April after the rainy season (Prov. 26:1). The wheat harvest of the highlands often continued into June, a hot season (Prov. 25:13). Great festivals and spiritual thanksgiving feasts were held at the close of the harvest (see Lev. 23:6, 10–14). What do the wise persons do at harvest (Prov. 10:5)? What do the foolish people do at harvest (Prov. 10:5)? (Hayford, J. W. 1997)

Activity 5: Create a Mind Map

Make a mind map about wisdom literature. Use sheets of unlined paper and colored markers or pencils. Draw a circle for each of the five books of wisdom literature. Draw lines out from the center as you determine the major categories of information (suffering, love, etc.). Branch lines from these will hold key subtopics. Use different colors for each cluster of information. Continue branching until you are out of room. Ask yourself: who, what, where, when, and how. Color and patterns will organize your ideas into meaningful groups which will make connections, associations, and relationships more clear. Also use symbols, numbers, arrows, or other "doodles" on your mind map. Do you see a pattern forming?

Activity 6: Discuss

Proverbs is written for instruction. Read and discuss the following passages and describe what happens: (1) when we behave wisely, and (2) when we behave unwisely.

1. Prov. 13:1, 15
2. Prov. 13:4
3. Prov. 13:7, 8
4. Prov. 13:17
5. Prov. 13:18

Step 4: Excel

Share your outline from Step 3 with a friend or family member. Explain what you have learned about the five books of wisdom literature.

Wisdom of Solomon   LS10114

Step 1: Excite

The Bible tells us that Solomon's desire for wisdom pleased God. In 1 Kings 3, we read the story of how Solomon asked God for wisdom. In verse 5, we find out that God appeared to him in a dream and asked him what he wanted God to give to him. Solomon asked for wisdom, and a portion of God's response to that request is found is verses 11–13.

> *Then God said to him: "Because you have asked this thing, and have not asked long life for yourself, nor have asked riches for yourself, nor have asked the life of your enemies, but have asked for yourself understanding to discern justice, behold, I have done according to your words; see, I have given you a wise and understanding heart, so that there has not been anyone like you before you, nor shall any like you arise after you. And I have also given you what you have not asked: both riches and honor, so that there shall not be anyone like you among the kings all your days."*

What does this tell you about God's desire for us to have wisdom? Think about Solomon's dream from God. What would you ask for if God appeared to you in such a dream? Why? Think about the implications your request would have on your own life and on the lives of those close to you if God were to grant your desire. Would your request be a wise one?

Step 2: Examine

Solomon was the third king of Israel (c. 971–931 B.C.), son of David and Bathsheba (2 Sam. 12:24). He built the first Temple in Jerusalem using forced labor and materials obtained from Hiram of Tyre. Solomon was Israel's first *dynastic* ruler. Saul and David, like the judges, were chosen because God had given them a special measure of power: They were *charismatic* rulers. Although Solomon took office without God's *charisma*, he received it during his vision at Gibeon when the Lord offered him his choice of gifts (1 Kings 3:5).

According to 1 Kings 4:32, Solomon wrote proverbs and songs. He was thought to have written many of the proverbial sayings and books. Among the works of the OT, Psalms 72 and 127, Proverbs, Song of Songs, and Ecclesiastes are ascribed to him. Much of the wisdom in Proverbs is said to be his, for example, Prov. 1:1; 10:1; 25:1. In Song of Songs he is often mentioned by name as the "bridegroom" and the "poet of love": 1:1,5; 3:7, 9, 11; 8:11.

Read 2 Chronicles chapters 1–9. This passage describes the reign of Solomon. After praying for wisdom, Solomon built and dedicated the Temple. His wealth and grandeur even impressed the Queen of Sheba.

The story of Solomon's prayer for wisdom is followed immediately in 1 Kings by that of two women who both claimed to be the mother of the same baby. When Solomon suggested that the living infant be divided, the true mother wept and was willing to give up her son, while the other readily agreed. Solomon's prayer for wisdom had been answered, and that answer made him able to help the true, deserving mother.

Recommended in: ♦ several lessons in this unit; ♥ several HOW unit studies.   ☛ Key Resource for this unit.

Suggested Resources

The following list contains more resources about Solomon.

Our Father Abraham: Jewish Roots of the Christian Faith ❖
"Solomon" (282).

Additional Reading

Lessons on Living from Solomon by Woodrow Kroll
This thirty-one day devotional from the Giants of the Old Testament series examines the rise and decline of a magnificent king who, despite his wisdom, allowed his passions to cloud his judgment. Let Solomon's life teach you that even great wisdom and wealth are meaningless apart from devotion and obedience to the Lord. Paperback - 65 pages (1999). Back To The Bible; ISBN: 0847406911.

Reflecting with Solomon by Roy Zuck
Reflecting With Solomon gathers some of the best scholarship on Ecclesiastes. The result is a solid introduction to Old Testament wisdom literature and more detail for study, preaching, and teaching than is found in most commentaries. Some articles cover the authorship, themes, difficulties, and overall structure in Ecclesiastes; others analyze specific texts. Paperback - 432 pages (1994). Baker/Revell; ISBN: 0801099390.

The Remarkable Wisdom of Solomon by Henry Morris
Inheriting and expanding a magnificent kingdom from his father, King David, Solomon attained both spiritual and material wealth, confounding his enemies and thrilling his own people. The Bible claims there will never be another like Him. His legacy includes three canonical works that flowed from God to his pen—Proverbs, Ecclesiastes, and Song of Solomon. Strangely, these three books are rarely examined by modern scholars, but longtime author and defender of the faith Henry Morris has now provided an invaluable commentary. His examination of Solomon's life, and the insights into the writings themselves, give the Bible student a worthy tour through the life of a most remarkable man. Paperback - 240 pages (2001). New Leaf Press (Master Books); ISBN: 0890513562.

The Wisdom of Solomon at Work by Charles C. Manz, Karen P. Manz, Robert Marx, Chris Neck
This book helps readers examine their own lives and work as they journey toward wisdom. Those with a Judeo-Christian background will reconnect with spiritual views, history, and symbols from the Old Testament. Those from other faith traditions will learn from stories about work and relationships that have withstood the test of time. The dramatic stories of Job, David, Ruth, Moses, and Solomon are drawn on to raise timeless questions of the human condition that have existed since biblical times. This book opens a valuable wisdom source that is relevant to contemporary work and life. Real-life stories—like that of Aaron Feuerstein, who risked his life savings to breathe life back into his company, and Malden Mills, after a devastating fire—show how spiritual wisdom can intersect with work life. Hardcover - 157 pages (2001) Berrett-Koehler Publishers; ISBN: 057675085X.

Video

Solomon: The Bible Collection Series
The ninth in a series of made-for-TV movies based on stories from the Bible, this drama stars Ben Cross as Solomon, the beloved son of David (Max Von Sydow), who inherits his father's kingdom and becomes the ruler of Israel. While Solomon consolidates power through his marriages, it is his intelligence, sense of justice, and desire to see his people live in peace that earns him the respect and admiration of his subjects. "Solomon" also stars Vivica A. Fox as the Queen of Sheba, Anouk Aimee as Bathsheba, and Maria Grazia Cucinotta as Abishag. 172 minutes. Video (2000) Chordant Distribution Group; ISBN: 8474024609.

Internet Source

King Solomon
Learn about the opposing forces that marked the reign of this Hebrew ruler who was renowned for his wisdom. Prepared for the Hebrew University of Jerusalem by Dana Barnea.
http://jeru.huji.ac.il/eb32s.htm

The Wisdom of Solomon
BIble study on 1 Kings 3:1-15.
http://www.congregationalchurch.org/biblestudy/bible020.htm

King Solomon
General information form Daily Bible Study.
http://www.keyway.ca/htm2002/solomon.htm

Step 3: Expand

Choose and complete one or more of the following activities:

Activity 1: Write a Letter
Many of the proverbs Solomon wrote are letters from a father to a son on godly, wise living. Write a letter as if you were a mother or father writing to your child. You should share from your heart the things you want them to know about life as they are growing up (minimum 300 words).

Activity 2: Make a Time Line
Make a visual time line of Solomon's life from conception to death. Mark and date every major event in his life. Make an oral presentation of your time line.

Activity 3: Find Solomon's Downfall
Read 1 Kings chapter 11. The Solomon presented here is different from the wise Solomon that we've looked at earlier. What sin did Solomon commit against God? What

---

Recommended in: ◆ several lessons in this unit; ● several HOW unit studies.   ●— Key Resource for this unit.

was the consequence for his unwise actions? Write a paper describing this time in Solomon's life, and how you can relate it to your life today. What lessons do you learn from this portion of Scripture? Refer to http://HeartofWisdom.com/Writing.htm.

Activity 4: Research and Write
Write an essay about the wisdom of Solomon. Be sure to include: the extent of wisdom, the extent of Solomon's kingdom, the peaceful life during Solomon's reign, examples of Solomon's great wisdom, the value of wisdom according to Solomon, where wisdom and knowledge come from, and how to gain wisdom. Refer to http://HeartofWisdom.com/Writing.htm.

Activity 5: Make a List
Ecclesiastes and Proverbs are expressions of a philosophy of life. Write down five statements which sum up important principles that should make up a Christian's character. Share with your parents and discuss the principles which can be applied in your life.

Step 4 Excel

Share the story of Solomon's wisdom with a younger person or your homeschool group. Be prepared to answer questions.

You can learn more about Solomon in Heart of Wisdom's *Ancient Israel: An Internet-Linked Unit Study*.

The Ultimate Wise Relationship LS10115

Step 1 Excite

Imagine that you died today and stood before God and He asked you, "Why should I let you into heaven?" What would you answer?

The Bible says that we are all sinners and fall short of the glory of God (Romans 3:23). Our sinful hearts refuse to let God be the Lord of our lives. Some people think that their good deeds will balance out their bad deeds. But the Bible never says that good deeds can pay for sins; sins; on the contrary, it says that our good deeds are as filthy rags in God's sight (Isa. 64:6).

Step 2 Examine

Biblical wisdom begins with a right relationship with God through Christ. The great message of the Bible about the Savior and God's plan of salvation for mankind. It is the gospel or good news of salvation. It is our relationship with the Messiah, Jesus Christ, that secures the sinner a personal work of redemption.

The believer's union with Jesus Christ is a *living* union. When we trusted Jesus Christ as our Savior, the Spirit of God gave us spiritual life and placed us into the body of Christ. *For by one Spirit are we all baptized into one body, whether we be Jews or Gentiles, whether we be bond or free* (1 Cor. 12:13). Notice that we did not put ourselves into his body, nor did another believer do it for us by means of some religious ritual. This work was totally and solely accomplished by the Holy Spirit of God in response to our faith in Christ (Wiersbe 1996).

There is only one way to to receive eternal life and get into heaven. No amount of good works or religious efforts can make a sinner holy. Only the blood of Jesus Christ can cleanse us from our sins (1 John 1:7). When we accept the free sacrifice Jesus made and make Jesus Lord of our lives, only then are we saved. Jesus said, *"No man can come to me, except the Father which hath sent me draw him: and I will raise him up at the last day"* (John 6:44). The salvation offered to all who believe is the same for everyone (Acts 16:31; Heb. 10:39). All the treasures of wisdom and knowledge are hidden in the person of the Messiah!

Many people know all about the Messiah, but few really *know* **Him**. Jesus desires to have a personal relationship with each of us. Wisdom is a by-product of that relationship. We don't seek Him for the wisdom He can give. We seek Him because He is the Messiah—because we desire to worship and adore Him. But as you begin to develop a relationship with Him, certain blessings and characteristics begin to well up in your life. Wisdom is one of those blessings. So remember that you should not only know *about* Him . . . you need to *know* Him.

Jesus is the Messiah prophesied in the Old Testament, and the one who is coming again. In Jesus is everything we need for life and godliness: love, joy, faith, healing, reconciliation, prosperity, and so on. And He is wisdom. When we turn to Him to help us through difficult decisions or times, He will be the

---

Recommended in: ◆ several lessons in this unit; ♥ several HOW unit studies.   ☞ Key Resource for this unit.

wisdom we need at any given hour. There are also times when we need wisdom that may not necessarily be "bad" times. When you become an adult, there will be many decisions involving jobs, investments, major purchases, and so on that are not trials or difficulties, but without God's wisdom these things can actually produce problems. Jesus has the wisdom we need for every situation, good or bad. He truly is our all in all!

Jesus' final words to His followers were in harmony with the focus of His life: "*Go ye therefore, and teach all nations, baptizing them in the name of the Father, and of the Son, and of the Holy Ghost: Teaching them to observe all things whatsoever I have commanded you: and, lo, I am with you always, even unto the end of the world. Amen*" (Matt. 28:19–20). This is the Great Commission to carry on with Jesus' task of teaching others. Our relationship with Christ is to continue to imitate Him and continue His ministry. To follow His example and to be His disciples, we must have the mind of Christ. To have the mind of Christ is to think like He does, to have His attitude toward life and people. As we learn to have the mind of Christ, the people around us will notice. In fact, people will be watching us to see how Christians handle responsibilities and trials.

Read and discuss the following verses:

Opening and alleging, that Christ must needs have suffered, and risen again from the dead; and that this Jesus, whom I preach unto you, is Christ. (Acts 17:3)

For I am not ashamed of the gospel of Christ: for it is the power of God unto salvation to every one that believeth; to the Jew first, and also to the Greek. (Rom. 1:16)

And all things are of God, who hath reconciled us to himself by Jesus Christ, and hath given to us the ministry of reconciliation; (2 Cor. 5:18)

But God, who is rich in mercy, for his great love wherewith he loved us, Even when we were dead in sins, hath quickened us together with Christ, (by grace ye are saved;) And hath raised us up together, and made us sit together in heavenly places in Christ Jesus: That in the ages to come he might shew the exceeding riches of his grace in his kindness toward us through Christ Jesus. For by grace are ye saved through faith; and that not of yourselves: it is the gift of God: Not of works, lest any man should boast. For we are his workmanship, created in Christ Jesus unto good works, which God hath before ordained that we should walk in them. (Eph. 2:4–10)

But we are bound to give thanks always to God for you, brethren beloved of the Lord, because God hath from the beginning chosen you to salvation through sanctification of the Spirit and belief of the truth: (2 Thess. 2:13)

Who hath saved us, and called us with an holy calling, not according to our works, but according to his own purpose and grace, which was given us in Christ Jesus before the world began. But is now made manifest by the appearing of our Saviour Jesus Christ, who hath abolished death, and hath brought life and immortality to light through the gospel: (2 Tim. 1:9–10)

For it became him, for whom are all things, and by whom are all things, in bringing many sons unto glory, to make the captain of their salvation perfect through sufferings. (Heb. 2:10)

Suggested Resources

Do more research. We recommend the following:

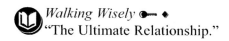

Walking Wisely ◉— ◆
"The Ultimate Relationship."

Our Father Abraham: Jewish Roots of the Christian Faith ♥
"Salvation: Escape or Involvement" (178–182; also see 14–14, 20–21, 42–43, 48–49, 90, 148–149, 231–232, 251).

Additional Reading

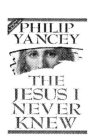

The Jesus I Never Knew by Philip Yancey
Philip Yancey realized that despite a lifetime of attending Sunday school, topped off by a Bible College education, he really had no idea who Jesus was. In fact, he found himself further and further removed from the person of Jesus, distracted instead by flannel-graph figures and intellectual inspection. He determined to use his journalistic talents to approach Jesus, in the context of time, within the framework of history. In *The Jesus I Never Knew*, Yancey explores the life of Jesus, as he explains, "'from below,' to grasp as best I can what it must have been like to observe in person the extraordinary events unfolding in Galilee and Judea" as Jesus traveled and taught. Yancey examines three fundamental questions: who Jesus was, why He came, and what He left behind. Step by step, scene by scene, Yancey probes the culture into which Jesus was born and grew to adulthood; His character and mission; His teachings and miracles; His legacy— not just as history has told it, but as He himself intended it to be. Hardcover - 288 pages (September 1995). Zondervan Publishing House; ISBN: 0310385709.

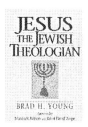

Jesus the Jewish Theologian by Brad Young, Marvin R. Wilson, David Wolpe
This book establishes Jesus firmly within the context of first-century Judaism and shows how understanding Jesus' Jewishness is crucial for interpreting the New Testament and for understanding the nature of the Christian faith. Paperback - 308 pages (November 1995). Hendrickson Publishers, Inc.; ISBN: 1565630602.
Reading level: college or adult.

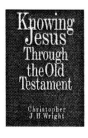

Knowing Jesus Through the Old Testament by Christopher J. H. Wright
Has the Christian Bible bound believers to a narrow and mistaken notion of Jesus? Christopher Wright proves that Jesus' own story is rooted in the story of Israel. Throughout his life, Jesus lived by the script of Israel. Only as we come to understand Jesus as a man with a story—an Old Testament story—will we come to know who Jesus truly is. To change that narrative is to deface our only reliable portrait of Jesus. Here is a

Recommended in: ◆ several lessons in this unit; ♥ several HOW unit studies.   ◉— Key Resource for this unit.

book that traces out the face of Christ in the textual tapestry of the Old Testament. But it also outlines the pattern of God's design for Israel as it is lived out in the story of Jesus. Paperback - 256 pages (1995). Intervarsity Pr; ISBN: 0830816933.

The Messiah: An Internet-Linked Unit Study by Robin Sampson
All the treasures of wisdom and knowledge are hidden in the person of the Messiah! This book gives you the opportunity to investigate ancient prophecies, hidden wisdom, things that people longed to know for centuries before the Messiah came to dwell on earth. We are in the privileged position of looking backward through history to see the Messiah as He was described in prophesy, as He dwelt on earth, as He is now, and as He speaks to us through His Word. (2001). Heart of Wisdom Publishing.

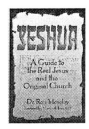

Yeshua: A Guide to the Real Jesus and Original Church by Ron Mosley
This is a well-researched and fascinating study of the Jewishness of the historical Jesus. The author explores the structure and mission of the original church in the Jewish culture of the first century. The book combines scholarship with an understandable writing style, resulting in a book that can be easily read but challenging to the reader. This book is a must for every serious student of the Bible in enlightening us as to our Jewish heritage. Forewords by Brad Young, Ph.D., Dr. Marvin Wilson, and Dwight Prior. Paperback - 213 pages (July 1998). Jewish New Testament Publishers; ISBN: 1880226685. Reading level: Grades 9 and up.

Video

That the World May Know by Ray Vander Laan
This powerful video series explores ancient Israel and its stunning relevance to our modern-day faith. Dr. James Dobson's visit to Israel changed his life. His guide and teacher, Ray Vander Laan, provided a rich combination of ancient history with modern lessons that brought the Scriptures to life as never before. James Dobson said, "Nothing has opened and illuminated the Scriptures for me quite like this presentation." It's a fascinating journey through landmarks of the Old and New Testaments. Available from Focus on the Family: (800) A-FAMILY (232-6459), http://www.family.org.

Internet Sources

Did Yeshua (Jesus) Claim To Be The Messiah?
Teaching article by Clarence H. Wagner from Bridges for Peace.
Jr.http://www.bridgesforpeace.com/publications/teaching/Article-45.html

I am the Bread of Life
Teaching Letter from Bridges for Peace.
http://bridgesforpeace.com/modules.php?name=News&file=article&sid=1499

(i) *Jesus' Education*
Article by David Bivin from JerusalemPerspective.com.
http://articles.jerusalemperspective.com/articles/DisplayArticle.aspx?ArticleID=1453

(i) *Jesus' Most Important Title*
Article by Randall Buth from JerusalemPerspective.com.
http://articles.jerusalemperspective.com/articles/DisplayArticle.aspx?ArticleID=1570

Step 3 Expand

Choose and complete one or more of the following activities:

Activity 1: Write a Paper
In Matthew 7:24–27, Jesus tells us about a wise man and a foolish man. Read these verses, and write a one-page paper about what Jesus taught in these verses. What do you think Jesus was trying to get across in this portion of Scripture?

Activity 2: Write Your Testimony
Write about your salvation experience as if you were writing to a child. Explain how you saw your need for a change in your life and the changes that occurred after the salvation experience.

Activity 3: Write a Letter to Jesus
Jesus was your age at one time. Write a letter to Him as a close personal friend. Thank Him for giving His life in place of yours. What would you choose to talk about in your letter? What types of questions would you ask Him?

Activity 4: Do Research
Luke 2:52 says: *And Jesus increased in wisdom and stature, and in favor with God and men.* Didn't He always have all wisdom, stature, and favor? How could He increase in these things? To better understand this concept, study the life of Jesus from conception to adulthood. In particular, locate Scriptures that demonstrate the human and childlike qualities of a young Jesus. Prepare a presentation on your findings, including a five-page paper, visual aids, and an oral presentation.

Activity 5: Write a Summary
Look up the verses below and write a summary on the four facts about salvation (Willmington, 1987).

> 1. Salvation is only produced by innocent blood (Heb. 9:22).
> 2. Salvation is always through a person (Acts 4:12;
>   1 Thess. 5:9; Heb. 5:9).
> 3. Salvation is always by grace (Eph. 2:8–9; Tit. 2:11).
> 4. Salvation is always through faith (Rom. 5:1; Heb. 11:6).

Activity 6: Research

Jesus is the prophesied Christ. Several Old Testament prophets foretold Jesus' birth, life, and death. Read each of the following prophecies and its fulfillment.

Prophecy	Old Testament	New Testament
Descendant of Abraham	Gen. 12:3	Matt. 1:1–17
Descendant of Isaac	Gen. 17:19	Luke 3:34
Descendant of Jacob	Num. 24:17	Matt. 1:2
From tribe of Judah	Gen. 49:10	Luke 3:33
Heir to throne of David	Isa. 9:7	Luke 1:32–33
Born in Bethlehem	Mic. 5:2	Luke 2:4–7
Time for His birth	Dan. 9:25	Luke 2:1–2
Born of a virgin	Isa. 7:14	Luke 1:26–31
Enters Jerusalem on a donkey	Zech. 9:9	Matt. 21:1–11

Step 4 Excel

Isa. 1:18–19 says, *"Come now, and let us reason together,"* says the Lord, *"Though your sins are like scarlet, they shall be as white as snow; though they are red like crimson, they shall be as wool. If you are willing and obedient, you shall eat the good of the land;"*

What do you think this Scripture refers to? Did you get a picture in your mind of the salvation that Jesus purchased for us when He died on the cross in our place?

Our sins were crimson, but God so loved the world that He allowed Jesus to die for us that we might be brought into right fellowship with God. The ultimate act of obedience to God is accepting the sacrifice of His Son, Jesus, for your sins. If you have never asked Jesus to come into your heart to forgive and save you, you can do that right now. Simply pray this prayer:

Dear God,

I believe that I am a sinner; that according to Your Word all have sinned and fallen short of Your glory. I believe that You love me so much that You sent Your Son, Jesus, to die for me. I also believe that You raised Him from the dead. The Bible says that if I believe in my heart and confess with my mouth, I will be saved. So, Jesus, I believe in my heart that You died for me. I accept Your sacrifice for my sins and I confess it with my mouth. Come into my heart, Lord Jesus, and save me. Be my Savior and help me to live each day for You. Teach me Your ways and help me resist sinful temptations. Amen.

If you prayed this prayer, tell a parent or your pastor. And congratulations—you've just been born into the kingdom of God! *He who has the Son has life; he who does not have the Son of God does not have life.* (1 John 5:12).

When you accept, by faith, that sin's power over you has been broken by Christ, you are free to become the person God wants you to be. You will no longer live for yourself. You should continually seek to live as Jesus would live, and trust Him to empower you and enable you to do so. Paul said, "*It is no longer I who live, but Christ lives in me*" (Gal. 2:20). Jesus said, "*I am the vine, you are the branches. He who abides in Me, and I in him, bears much fruit; for without Me you can do nothing...By this My Father is glorified, that you bear much fruit; so you will be My disciples* (John 15:5,8).

Continue your walk in prayer and Bible study to grow closer to God. Develop an intimate relationship with the Lord, listening to Him continually, and He will lead you to wisdom. Pray the prayer for yourself that Paul prayed for the Ephesians: That they might be given a "*spirit of wisdom and revelation in the knowledge of Him, the eyes of your understanding being enlightened so that they might know the hope of His calling, the riches of the glory of His inheritance, and the exceeding greatness of His power toward them*" (Eph. 1:17–18). Go and tell others of your relationship with Christ.

Works Cited

Achtemeier, P. J. 1985. *Harper's Bible Dictionary.* Includes index. (1st ed.) (Page 131). San Francisco: Harper & Row.

Blizzard, Roy. 1995. *Understanding the Difficult Words of Jesus: New Insights from a Hebraic Perspective.* Shippensburg, PA: Destiny Image.

Hayford, Jack. 1997, c1996. *Everyday Wisdom for Everlasting Life: A Study of Proverbs.* Spirit-Filled Life Bible Discovery Guides. Nashville: Thomas Nelson.

Henry, Matthew. 1996, c1991. *Matthew Henry's Commentary on the Whole Bible: Complete and Unabridged in One Volume.* (Prov. 1:7). Peabody: Hendrickson Publishers.

Karleen, Paul. 1987. *The Handbook to Bible Study: With a Guide to the Scofield Study System.* "This book is intended as a companion to the Scofield Reference Bible"--Pref.; Includes indexes. New York: Oxford University Press.

MacArthur, John. 1997, c1992. *Rediscovering Expository Preaching.* (Page 120). Dallas: Word Pub.

Manz, C.C., K.P. Manz, R.D. Marx, and C.P. Neck. 2001. *The Wisdom of Solomon at Work: Ancient Virtues for Living and Leading Today.* San Francisco: Berrett-Koehler Publishers.

Mosley, Ron. 1995. *The Spirit of the Law.* Hagerstown, MD: Edbed Publishing.

Overman, Christian. 1996. *Assumptions that Affect Our Lives.* Simi Valley, CA: Micah 6:8 Publishing.

Peterson, E. H. 1995. *The Message: New Testament with Psalms and Proverbs.* (Prov. 1:1). Colorado Springs, CO: NavPress.

Pfeiffer, C. F. 1962. *The Wycliffe Bible Commentary: New Testament.* (Matt. 7:24). Chicago: Moody Press.

Richards, L. 1991. *The Bible Reader's Companion.* (Prov. 1:1). Wheaton, IL: Victor Books.

Sampson, Robin. 2001. *Ancient History: Adam to Messiah.* Woodbridge, VA: Heart of Wisdom Publishing.

_____. 2001. *What Your Child Needs to Know When.* Woodbridge, VA: Heart of Wisdom Publishing.

Smith, James E. 1996. The Wisdom Literature and Psalms. Joplin, MO: College Press Pub. Co.

Stern, David. 1992. *Jewish New Testament Commentary: A Companion Volume to the Jewish New Testament.* (Rom. 13:8). Clarksville, MD: Jewish New Testament Publications.

Waltke, Bruce K. 2000. *The Way of Wisdom.* Grand Rapids, MI: Zondervan Publishing House.

Walvoord, J. F. 1983, c1985. *The Bible Knowledge Commentary: An Exposition of the Scriptures.* (Prov. 13:20). Wheaton, IL: Victor Books.

Wiersbe, Warren W. 1993. *Wiersbe's Expository Outlines on the Old Testament.* (Prov. 12:1). Wheaton, IL: Victor Books.

_____. 1996, c1988. *Be What You Are: 12 Intriguing Pictures of the Christian from the New Testament.* (Pages 51–52). Wheaton, IL: Tyndale House.

_____.1996, c1995. *Be Skillful. An Old Testament Study.* (Prov. 3:1). Wheaton, IL: Victor Books.

Willmington, Harold L. 1987. *Willmington's Book of Bible Lists.* Wheaton, IL: Tyndale House.

Wood, Douglas. 1996. *New Bible Dictionary.* (3rd ed.) (Page 842). Leicester, England; Downers Grove, IL: InterVarsity Press.

Printed in the United States
33109LVS00003B/305-326

9 780970 181664